THE ROUGH GUIDE TO

Family Fun
in Ireland

written and researched by

Geoff Wallis and Ben West

ROUGH
GUIDES

Credits

Editorial: Helena Smith
Layout: Katie Stephens
Proofreading: Carole Mansur
Production: Julia Bovis
Cover: David Wearn
Cartography: Katie Lloyd-Jones

Project managed by Remote World Ltd

Publishing Information

Published April 2005 by Rough Guides Ltd,
80 Strand, London WC2R 0RL

© Rough Guides 2005

ISBN 1843535556

Printed in Italy by LegoPrint S.p.A

A catalogue record for this book is available from the British Library

Contents

Introduction

The island of Ireland may not seem the most obvious place to take your family on holiday, but in fact both North and South have plenty for families, whether it involves exploring the countryside, cruising on the extensive Shannon-Erne waterway, taking in the big city life of Dublin, Cork, Galway or Belfast, or just sitting back and enjoying the atmosphere of a cosy country pub. There are amazing archaeological sites such as Newgrange and Dún Aengus, and dramatic, often stunning landscapes like the Giant's Causeway and the Burren. Children are well catered for, through the number of attractions geared to their interests, and a host of possible outdoor activities from riding, angling and sailing to canoes, go-karts and mountain-bike trails. Virtually every village has its summer festival, with many providing activities and events for families, while Ireland's arts are thriving and lively and you'll never be too far away from a cinema, theatre or musical venue – indeed, traditional music is one of the things kids most enjoy.

There's great wildlife as well: Ireland is a birdwatcher's paradise, inhabited by a host of native and migratory birds, especially around the coast and inland waters, and you might even be lucky to spot schools of dolphins or the occasional whale basking in inshore waters. Above all, Ireland is renowned for its hospitality and friendliness: wherever you go, you and your family will be made to feel welcome. Only the weather can't be relied upon, and although the temperatures are often milder than you might expect – due to the effects of the Gulf Stream – there can be rain at any time of year. Bring rainwear, just in case.

Accommodation

Both North and South Ireland offer possibilities to suit every budget, from luxurious hotels to the pleasures of camping or touring the country in a rented gypsy caravan. Whatever your choice, bear in mind that accommodation can be difficult to find at the time of festivals, during public holiday weekends and in the cities and major tourist areas during July and August. Fortunately, the majority of tourist offices can book you accommodation for a small fee, and there are also plenty of ways to book online. We've listed a few recommendations in the text, but bear in mind that these are just a selection – comprehensive guides are available from Tourism Ireland.

Many hotels, especially in the cities, offer a range of special deals, particularly at weekends, while others, such as the *Jurys Inns* chain, charge a price for a room, rather than per person, offering an economical choice for families. Welcoming B&Bs can be found everywhere in Ireland, most providing the traditional huge Irish breakfast, while many also have at least one room for overnight family accommodation. Below these in price are hostels, which fall into two categories – the official ones run by An Óige in the Republic and Hostelling International Northern Ireland, and the independents, many of which are members of either or both the Independent Holiday Hostels of Ireland Association or Independent Hostels Ireland. Most hostels have rooms suitable for families.

Campsites can be found all around Ireland's coastline with many inland, too, especially in popular tourist areas. Most are well equipped and offer facilities such as children's play areas. Self-catering can be a very economical option, or you can rent a boat and go cruising on one of Ireland's inland waterways – several holiday companies specialize in this area.

Sports and activities

Birdwatching

Ireland's west and north coasts, especially islands such as Clear and Rathlin, offer the best opportunities for observing sea birds. Strangford Lough in Northern Ireland and the Wexford Slobs in the Republic's southeast are wintering grounds for various species of migratory birds. The mud flats of the east and south are home to thousands of waders and wildfowl. There's also the chance to see rare birds such as the chough in the west and the corncrake in Donegal.

Cycling

Ireland now has more than twenty waymarked cycling trails, varying in length from relatively short circuits like the Glens of Antrim Trail to more arduous, long-distance routes including the Wicklow and Wexford Tour. Details of these, cycling-holiday tour companies and other information useful to cyclists can be found in the Tourism Ireland brochure,

Cycling in Ireland. Details of bike rental outlets can be found in each chapter of this guide.

Fishing

Hundreds of lakes and rivers provide opportunities for fly- and game-fishing. Local tourist offices can provide details of the best spots and inform you where you can get a coarse- or game-fishing licence and a permit from the water's owner. Virtually every port or harbour in Ireland has boats offering sea-angling trips. Tourism Ireland publishes a handy brochure.

Gaelic football, hurling and camogie

Hurling is a fast, tough and skilful fifteen-a-side game played with a wooden hurley stick (*camán*) and a leather ball (*sliotar*) where the aim is to strike the ball into the net to score three points or hit it over the crossbar of posts similar to those in rugby to score one point. This game (and camogie, the women's version) is well worth catching. The season runs from the early summer to September and the counties where these games are most popular include Clare, Cork, Kilkenny, Offaly and Tipperary. Gaelic football shares the same pitches, scoring system and team-size as hurling, and bears similarities to both association football and rugby in that the ball can be kicked, caught and hand-passed (as in volleyball), while players can run with the ball as long as they tap it from foot to hand. It is now more popular than hurling, and games can be found throughout the country during the summer. For details of fixtures visit Ⓦwww.gaa.ie.

Golf and pitch and putt

Ireland's golf courses can be among the most challenging – and scenic – in the world. Tourist offices can supply the details and there are a number of companies specializing in golfing holidays. There are plenty of pitch and putt courses, too, which younger talents will enjoy, and details of these are provided in this guide. Tourism Ireland also publishes a useful brochure.

Horse riding and horse racing

The Irish love horses (and they love betting on them too). We've listed in each chapter the numerous opportunities for riding and trekking provided by equestrian centres. For those who love a flutter, there are plenty of race meetings and we've also provided details of the main courses.

Walking

Ireland has waymarked long-distance trails (visit Ⓦwww.irishwaymarkedways.ie for details) as well as innumerable shorter walks across a variety of different terrains, though many of the best involve hill- and mountain-walking or traversing blustery coastal paths. There are good guidebooks to help you plan longer walks, and many local tourist offices and local councils produce their own guides to walks in their area.

Water sports

Over three thousand miles of coastline, many glorious beaches and myriad lakes, rivers and other waterways offer a host of opportunities for surfing, windsurfing, water-skiing or diving and getting out on the water in a yacht, canoe, kayak or rowing boat. Again, Tourism Ireland publishes a booklet detailing the many companies offering water-based activities, *Watersports in Ireland*. A clean coastline makes swimming a pleasure, too, but beware of tides and dangerous undercurrents. Fortunately, the number of indoor swimming pools, especially family-oriented centres, has increased significantly, offering safe conditions whatever the weather.

Costs and money

Gone are the days when the Republic of Ireland was a low-cost holiday destination. Over the last few years the price of tourist essentials, such as transport and eating out, has risen. However, it is still possible for the budget-conscious family to enjoy the country to the full. Away from the major tourist areas you'll also find that your budget tends to stretch a lot further. Whereas the opposite used to be the case, Northern Ireland can now be a considerably cheaper place to visit than the Republic, with the exception of the cost of petrol.

Discount cards

If you're intending to visit plenty of historic monuments, it's worth considering purchasing a discount card. In the Republic many buildings, monuments and parks are run by Dúchas, the Heritage Service (℡01/647 2453, ⓦwww .heritageireland.ie). It offers a yearly family Heritage Card for €50 which provides unlimited admission to all of its sites. In Northern Ireland, the National Trust (℡0870/458 4000) has a comparable deal with a family membership ticket costing £65. Although it covers far fewer attractions than Dúchas, members are also entitled to free entry to Trust properties in the rest of the UK and reduced admission prices to Dúchas sites. We've indicated in the chapters which facilities are run by Dúchas or the National Trust.

Getting around

If you're driving your own car to Ireland, you must have a current driving licence (visitors from non-EU countries also need an International Driving Permit) and should also check that your insurance policy covers your trip; bring your vehicle registration or ownership document too. Most road signs give the place names in both Irish and English, but in Gaeltacht (Irish-speaking) areas, the names may appear only in Irish and be very different from the English version, so make sure you have a good map. Speed limits on Irish roads have changed from miles to kilometres per hour. There are five kinds: town and city (50km/h); national road (100km/h); regional and local (80km/h); motorway (120km/h); and special (30km/h or 60km/h).

If you're reliant solely upon public transport and planning to travel around Ireland, the Republic's Bus Éireann (@www.buseireann.ie) and Iarnród Éireann (@www.irishrail.ie) and the North's Ulsterbus and Northern Ireland Railways (both @www.transco.uk) offer a variety of travel passes (children half-price). You can also fly between Dublin and Cork (Aer Arann, @www.aerarann.com; Aer Lingus, @www.aerlingus.com), Belfast and Cork (Aer Arann), Dublin and Donegal, Kerry, Knock, Galway and Sligo (Aer Arann), and Dublin and Derry (Logan Air, @www.ba.com).

Finally, cycling can be one of the most pleasant ways to explore Ireland, though it's advisable to stay well clear of the major trunk roads and avoid Dublin entirely. It's quite easy to rent a bike in the Republic, though there are far fewer rental outlets in the North. Be aware that many Irish dogs regard bicycles (and often cars too) as fair game for a chase!

Food and drink

The range and quality of Ireland's cafés and restaurants have increased markedly over the last decade. Indeed, just about anywhere in the Republic and the North you'll be hard-pressed not to be able to find a decent meal. Many pubs also

Spot that number

Driving around the Republic of Ireland, you'll notice that virtually every car number plate includes a letter or pair of letters indicating where it was registered. Each car number plate has three parts: the date, the county and the registration number itself, e.g. 93–DL–12345 would mean that the car was the 12,345th to be registered in County Donegal in 1993. There are 26 counties in the Republic, but Tipperary has two different pairs of letters and there are separate codes for the cities and counties of Limerick and Waterford, making 29 different index marks altogether. See how many you can spot. Dublin will be easy, but spying a number plate from a county with a small population (such as Leitrim or Roscommon) might be tricky. So keep your eyes peeled.

C – Cork	LS – Laois
CE – Clare	MH – Meath
CN – Cavan	MN – Monaghan
CW – Carlow	MO – Mayo
D – Dublin	OY – Offaly
DL – Donegal	RN – Roscommon
G – Galway	SO – Sligo
KE – Kildare	TN – Tipperary North
KK – Kilkenny	TS – Tipperary South
KY – Kerry	W – Waterford City
L – Limerick City	WD – Waterford County
LD – Longford	WH – Westmeath
LH – Louth	WW – Wicklow
LK – Limerick County	WX – Wexford
LM – Leitrim	

now serve food, throughout the day. Outside the larger places, the pub lunch staple is usually meat and two veg, plus plenty of potatoes, though many pubs are branching out in their menu choices. If you're staying in B&Bs, you'll usually be served the filling "traditional" Irish cooked breakfast, consisting of sausages, bacon and eggs, often with a variety of different breads.

The pub is still the social focus throughout Ireland. In the Republic, opening hours are Monday to Thursday 10.30am to 11.30pm, Friday and Saturday 10.30am to 12.30am and Sunday 12.30 to 11.30pm. In the North the opening times are Monday to Saturday 11.30am to 11pm and Sunday 12.30 to 10pm. Irish pubs are renowned for the "craic", that invigorating mixture of conversation and laughter, often spiced by a traditional music session. You'll find such sessions all year round in large towns and the cities and some traditional music havens, though in many rural areas you'll only be likely to catch a session between June and September. Most do not begin until at least 9.30pm (and often later), though a few pubs have Sunday afternoon sessions. Unfortunately, though most pubs are generally very welcoming to children, new legislation has barred anyone under the age of 18 from being in a pub after 9pm.

Festivals

Virtually every town and many villages have a festival of some kind at some point during the summer, many taking place over the June or August public holidays (local tourist offices will have the details). Many of these can be great fun for families, offering plenty of child-oriented events. Tourism Ireland publishes a useful Calendar of Events.

St Patrick's Day March 17 ⓦwww.stpatricksfestival.ie. Celebrations all over Ireland, including parades and events, ranging from an annual horse-ploughing competition in Ballycastle, Co. Antrim, to a full week of activities in Dublin.

World Irish Dancing Championships Easter ⓦwww .clrg.ie. Spread over seven days and held at different locations annually. The 2005 championship is in Ennis.

North West 200 Mid-May ⓣ028/7772 9869. Ireland's top motorcycle race takes place on a scenic circuit around Portrush, Co. Antrim.

Fleadh Nua Late May ⓦwww.fleadhnua.com. Ennis, Co. Clare, hosts this major traditional music festival.

Medaza May 28–30 ⓣ021/4355152, ⓦwww.medaza.com. Three days of world-class entertainment from hot-air balloons to a whole village of bouncy castles and huge inflatable slides.

Killarney Summerfest Late June/early July ⓦwww .killarneysummerfest.com. A major family festival in Co. Kerry.

Willie Clancy Summer School of Traditional Music Early July ⓦwww.setdancingnews.net. Hugely popular traditional music festival, held in Miltown Malbay, Co. Clare.

Galway Arts Festival Mid- to late July ⓦwww .galwayartsfestival.com. Massive festival with plenty of fun for families.

Mary from Dungloe Late July/early Aug ⓦwww .maryfromdungloe.info. Ten days of fun, frolics and music in Dungloe, Co. Donegal, culminating in the selection of "Mary", and a concert by Daniel O'Donnell.

Irish place names

Almost every Irish place name refers to some feature of the natural or built landscape and, as you tour the country, you'll keep encountering names which share certain elements. The Anglicized versions of the original often run together parts of the name and frequently change the spelling, so Arboe originated as Ard Bó, Ballycastle as Baile Chaisleáin, Killashandra as Cill na Seanrátha, and so on. Once you know some of the elements, it can be simple to work out what the place name means; for example, Bunbeg is "the little foot of the river". Many places also incorporate the name, so Inishowen comes from Inis Eoghain and means "Owen's peninsula". We've listed some of the most common below with their usual English renditions in brackets. See how many you can spot.

abhainn (avin or arvan) – river

achadh (agha) – field

ard – height

áth – ford

baile (bally) – townland, farmstead, territory

bán – white

beag (beg) – little

béal (bally or bel) – (ford) mouth

beann (ben) – peak, summit, cliff

bó – cow

bún – bottom, foot (of a river)

carn (cairn) – cairn

carraig (carrick) – rock

ceann (kin or ken) – headland

cill (kil or kill) – church

creágan (creggan) – rocky place

cloch – stone

doire (derry) – oak-wood

droim or dromainn (drum) – ridge

dubh (dub) – black

dún – fort

eas (as, ass or es) – waterfall

fionn (fin or finn) – white, fair, bright

gall (gal) – foreigner

glas (glass) – green, grey or stream.

gleann (glen) – glen or valley

inis (innis, inish, ennis, etc) – island, peninsula or river-meadow

linn (lin) – pool

má (magh) – plain

mór (more) – big

muc (muck) – pig

muine (money) – thicket

ráth – ring-fort

rós (ross) – wood or headland

sean (shan) – old

sliabh (slieve) – mountain

sneachta (snaght) – snow

tír (tyr) – land

trá – strand, beach

Ballyshannon Folk and Traditional Music Festival
Early Aug ⓦ www.ballyshannonfolkfestival.com. Lots of music and family entertainment in South Donegal.

Puck Fair Mid-Aug ⓦ www.puckfair.ie. Killorglin's annual traditional fair and festival attracts participants from way beyond County Kerry's borders, especially to see a goat enthroned as king of the town.

Kilkenny Arts Festival Mid-Aug ⓦ www.kilkennyarts.ie. Major ten-day festival including many events for children.

Fleadh Cheoil na hÉireann Late Aug ⓦ www.comhaltas.com. Huge traditional music festival held more often than not in Listowel, Co. Kerry.

Rose of Tralee International Festival Late Aug ⓦ www .roseoftralee.ie. Huge festival culminating in the crowning of the Rose in Tralee, Co. Kerry.

Oul' Lammas Fair Late Aug ⓣ 028/2076 2024. Ballycastle, Co. Antrim, hosts Ireland's oldest traditional market fair with plenty of street entertainment.

Hallowe'en Late Oct. Events all over Ireland but none surpasses the week of entertainment, merriment and mayhem in Derry (ⓦ www.derrycity.gov.uk/halloween).

Fairies, legends and place names

Everybody loves a story, but probably none more so than the Irish. Indeed, the role of the *shanachie* (or storyteller) was an important part of Irish communities until recent times. Fairies play a major part in Irish legend. There are places named after them, such as the hills Sheemore and Sheebeag in County Leitrim, which literally mean "Hill of the Big Fairies" and "Hill of the Little Fairies". The banshee, which means "woman of the fairy-mound", is a rather macabre spirit who wails to warn of the imminent death of someone. The best-known fairies, of course, are the leprechauns, notorious for having a crock of gold in their possession, but, if you see one, you're unlikely to have time to lay your hands on his riches. Fairies were also thought to have the gift of song and music and there's many a tale of a musician, who walked into a fairy ring knowing just a few tunes and came out with a repertoire large enough to keep people dancing all night.

1

Dublin

et around the gorgeous sweep of Dublin Bay and divided by the River Liffey, Ireland's capital is a vibrant, thriving place with plenty to offer families. There's an abundance of attractions, including museums, castles, historic

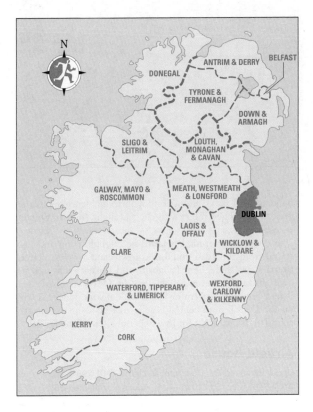

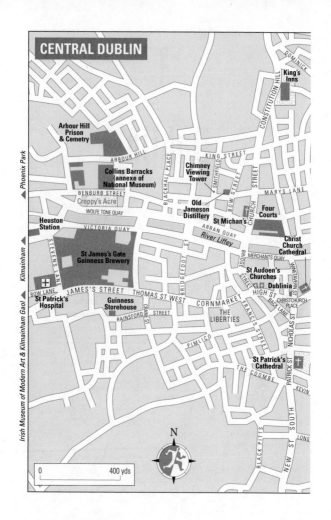

CENTRAL DUBLIN

Phoenix Park
Irish Museum of Modern Art & Kilmainham Gaol ◄ Kilmainham ◄
DOMINICK
King's Inns
CONSTITUTION HILL
Arbour Hill Prison & Cemetry
ARBOUR HILL
KING STREET
BLACKHALL PLACE
Chimney Viewing Tower
SMITHFIELD
BOW STREET
CHURCH STREET
MARYS LANE
Collins Barracks (annexe of National Museum)
BENBURB STREET
Croppy's Acre
WOLFE TONE QUAY
Old Jameson Distillery
St Michan's Church
Four Courts
Heuston Station
VICTORIA QUAY
ARRAN QUAY
River Liffey
Christ Church Cathedral
STEVENS LANE
St James's Gate Guinness Brewery
BRIDGEFOOT ST
MERCHANTS QUAY
St Audoen's Churches
WINETAVERN ST
Dublinia
CHRISTCHURCH PLACE
BOW LANE
St Patrick's Hospital
JAMES'S STREET
THOMAS ST WEST
CORNMARKET
HIGH ST
BACK LANE
NICHOLAS ST
Guinness Storehouse
CRANE ST
THE LIBERTIES
FRANCIS STREET
RAINSFORD STREET
PIMLICO
St Patrick's Cathedral
THE COOMBE
PATRICK ST
KEVIN
BLACK PITTS
NEW ST
SOUTH
LONG
N
0   400 yds

buildings and parks, and a cosmopolitan ambience about the place which draws the crowds day and night. Most of Dublin is readily navigable on foot or by the excellent bus service. The countryside around is farmland, though along and just inland from the coast you'll find towns and villages such as Skerries, Malahide, Dún Laoghaire and Dalkey, each with its own attractions, and explorable via the DART (Dublin Area Rapid Transport) system or urban rail network. Indeed, a trip on the DART from central Dublin to Killiney is well worth taking in its own right for its wonderful vistas of Dublin Bay.

Airfield House

Upper Kilmacud Rd, Dundrum, Dublin 14 ☎ 01/298 4301.
April–Sept Tues–Sun 10am–4pm. Adults €5, children €3.

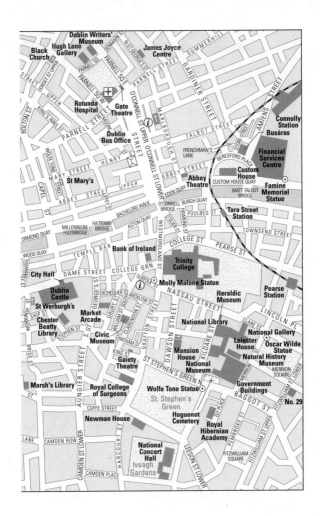

The nineteenth-century Airfield House and its forty-acre estate was once owned by the Overend sisters, famous for driving around Dublin in their Rolls-Royce (now in the house's vintage car museum). All now belongs to the Airfield Trust which uses the house for exhibitions and musical events. There's a farm where you can see animals such as goats, cows and horses, alongside ducks and hens (a farmers' market is held here every Friday) as well as formal gardens, a picnic area and outdoor café.

The Ark

11A Eustace St, Dublin 2 ⓣ 01/670 7788, ⓦ www.ark.ie.
Opening times and charges depend upon the programme.
The Ark is a custom-built cultural centre offering an inno-

vative programme of arts activities designed with children in mind (and often involving children in its development). Focusing on participation and interaction, the Ark mounts all manner of events geared towards specific age groups, including plays, exhibitions, workshops, concerts, readings and dance.

The Bram Stoker Dracula Experience

Bar Code, Westwood Club, Clontarf Rd, Dublin 3 Ⓣ 01/805 7824, Ⓦ www.thebramstokerdraculaexperience.com. Fri–Sun hourly noon–10pm. Adults €7, children €4, family €20.

Bram Stoker, the Dublin-born author of the classic horror tale, *Dracula*, lived at 15 The Crescent, very near this new hi-tech centre devoted to both his life and his spine-tingling work. Boasting animatronic models and props, and employing one hundred gallons of imitation blood, the tour takes visitors through the Time Tunnel to Transylvania and into Dracula's Castle, where the vampire himself rests in his coffin. All should be hugely entertaining for your little horrors, but perhaps a little too realistic for the very young.

Information

The main Tourism Centre (Ⓦ www.visitdublin.com) is on Suffolk Street, Dublin 2, with other branches at 14 O'Connell Street Upper, Dublin 1, the arrivals hall at Dublin Airport and the Dún Laoghaire Ferry Terminal; telephone contact can be made only through the freephone number – Ⓣ 1800/668 668/within Ireland Ⓣ 1850/230 330 – which provides information on the city's events and attractions. The free fortnightly newspaper *The Event Guide* (Ⓦ www.eventguide.ie) provides detailed listings of events, exhibitions and entertainment. Cinema and theatre listings appear in the daily *Irish Times* and *Evening Herald*.

The Chimney Viewing Tower

Smithfield village, Dublin 7 ℡ 01/817 3800,
Ⓦ www.chiefoneills.com. Mon–Sat 10am–5.30pm, Sun
11am–5.30pm. Adults €5, children €3.50, family €10.
Simply taking a trip up the side of the old Jameson Distillery
chimney is exciting; a glass-panelled lift whisks you 185ft to
the viewing platform. The panoramic view of the city and
its countryside from here is unmatched and unforgettable.

Dublin Zoo

Phoenix Park, Dublin 8 ℡ 01/474 8900, Ⓦ www.dublinzoo.ie.
March–Sept Mon–Sat 9.30am–6pm, Sun 10.30am–6pm;
Oct–Feb Mon–Sat 9.30am–dusk, Sun 10.30am–dusk. Adults
€13, children under 16 €8.50 (under 3s free), family €36–45.
A trip to the zoo is always popular with the little ones, but
what makes Dublin Zoo special is its concentration on breeding rare and endangered species for release into the wild –
with the resulting new-born arrivals offering regular photo

Open-top bus tours and bus passes

One of the most enjoyable ways to explore Dublin is to take an
open-top bus tour around the centre (for a watery alternative
see p.23). Tickets for tours last for 24 hours from the time of
first use, allow passengers to join the tour and hop on and hop
off at selected stops around the city, and give discounts to
admission prices at the various attractions along the route.
Tickets can be purchased from the addresses below, from
tourism centres, from the bus driver or online.

Dublin Bus 59 O'Connell St Upper, Dublin 1 ℡ 01/873 4222,
Ⓦ www.dublinbus.ie. Tours run every day of the year at ten-
minute intervals 9.30am–5pm and every thirty minutes
5–6.30pm, commencing from outside the company office.
Commentary is provided by often very witty (and sometimes
even singing) drivers. Adults €12.50, children €6. As an alternative for the independently minded, Dublin Bus offers a number of
different travel passes. The **Family One-Day Rambler** costs
€7.50. There's also a variety of **Adult Rambler** passes ranging
from one day (€5) to seven days (€18). Children under 16 can
get a seven-day **Travelwide pass** (€5), though those over 12
require a Schoolchild Photo ID from the Dublin Bus office.

Irish City Tours 33–34 Bachelors Walk, Dublin 1 ℡ 01/782
9010, Ⓦ www.irishcitytours.com. Daily tours every fifteen minutes from 9.30am with the last tour leaving at 5.30pm from mid-
July to Sept, 5pm from April to mid-July and during Oct, and
4pm Nov–March (adults €14, children €5, family €32). Tours
commence from outside 14 O'Connell Street Upper and commentary is given by an expert guide.

opportunities. More photo-ops are to be had on the zoo's City Farm, where children are welcome to pet and cuddle some of the more mundane of the over seven hundred species of animals and birds represented at Phoenix Park, whose other attractions include an expansive African Plains section, plenty of big cats and primates, sea lions and penguins.

Dublinia

St Michael's Hill, Christchurch, Dublin 8 ⊤ 01/679 4611, Ⓦ www.dublinia.ie. April–Sept daily 10am–5pm; Oct–March Mon–Sat 11am–4pm. Adults €6, children €3.50, family €15.

Dublinia's intention is to bring to life the streets of medieval Dublin and the people who bustled about them, and to a large extent it succeeds with a great deal of fun. Before you enter make sure to persuade someone to photograph you in the stocks outside the building. Inside you'll discover various shops and stalls where you can ogle the pies, try on clothes and have a go at brass rubbing, not forgetting to test your throwing skills at another set of stocks. You can marvel, too, at a rather gruesome Black Death tableau before examining some of the findings from the excavations of Wood Quay, including human and animal remains. Finally, there's a steep climb to the top of St Michael's Tower for a view of the surrounding area (albeit through rather grubby windowpanes).

The GAA Museum

Croke Park, Dublin 3 ⊤ 01/819 2323, Ⓦ www.gaa.ie. Mon–Sat 9.30am–5pm, Sun noon–5pm (closed on match days). Adults €5.50, children €3.50, family €15 (including stadium tour adults €9.50, children €6, family €24).

Croke Park is the headquarters of the Gaelic Athletic Association and a stadium whose capacity of more than 80,000 spectators makes it the fourth largest in Europe. Housed under the main stand, its excellent museum takes you through the history of the sports of hurling and Gaelic football, offering enthralling displays and plenty of touch-screen interaction. Best of all, however, are the chances to try your skills at whacking a *sliotar* (hurling ball) with a *camán* (hurling stick) and testing your reactions at catching a ball.

Guinness Storehouse

St James's Gate, Dublin 8 ⊤ 01/408 4800, Ⓦ www .guinness-storehouse.com. Daily 9.30am–5pm. Adults €14, children aged 6–12 €5 (under 6s free), family €30.

Even if your children haven't driven you to drink, you should bring them here; it's a seven-storey temple to all things connected with the black stuff (more than two and a half million pints of which are produced daily) that takes visitors on a self-guided trip through the drink's manufacturing process, replete with cascades of water, vast barrels and a surviving engine from the plant's old railway. It's a thoroughly noisy, gargantuan place which gives children a real and fun insight into the reason their parents are always thirsty in Ireland.

The second floor houses a collection of memorabilia, including advertisements both old and more recent (including a fascinating selection of comic videos) and also the eighteenth-century Downhill Harp, a version of the classic brass-strung instrument on which the Guinness logo is based. Tours end at the seventh-floor *Gravity Bar* which offers not only a pint of what some reckon to be the best Guinness in Dublin (included in the admission price, for those over 18) but a stunning panorama of the city and surrounding countryside.

Irish Museum of Modern Art

Royal Hospital, Military Rd, Kilmainham, Dublin 8 ⓣ 01/612 9900, ⓦ www.imma.ie. Tues–Sat 10am–5.30pm, Sun noon–5.30pm. Free.

Housed in the seventeenth-century Royal Hospital, set in splendid grounds, the museum hosts a varied programme of exhibitions, some of which may be of interest to older children. On Sundays (2–5pm; free) IMMA offers drop-in art exploration sessions for families, involving a range of different art-making projects.

Kilmainham Gaol

Inchicore Rd, Kilmainham, Dublin 8 ⓣ 01/453 5984, ⓦ www .heritageireland.ie. April–Sept daily 9.30am–5pm; Oct–March Mon–Sat 9.30am–4pm, Sun 10am–5pm. Adults €5, children €2, family €11. Heritage Card.

One of the most startling visitor attractions in the whole of Ireland, Kilmainham Gaol functioned as a rigorous house of punishment and correction from 1796 to 1924. Its notoriety lies in the fact that leaders of every Irish rebellion between 1798 and 1916 were incarcerated here, while the last prisoner to be released was Eamon de Valera in 1924, subsequently to become Ireland's Taoiseach (prime minister) and later its president. Guided tours take place every 45 minutes, so, if you're early, do make sure to take in the gaol's fascinating exhibition which provides much background information on how the prison was run, prisoners' conditions, nineteenth-century crime (including an early "mugshot" camera) and the various struggles for independence.

The tour itself takes in the tiers of cells which form the East Wing, the prison Chapel and the harsh and cramped conditions of the West Wing, together with a short but evocative video on the prison's history and the yacht *Asgard*, used by Erskine Childers and his sister Molly to smuggle guns into Ireland in 1914. Bear in mind that there was no heating in the prison and there still isn't, so wrap up well if you're visiting in winter.

Lambert Puppet Theatre

5 Clifton Lane, Monkstown, Co. Dublin ⓣ01/280 0964,
ⓦwww.lambertpuppettheatre.com.
This theatre stages daily shows during May and June (call for times) and all-year performances on Saturdays and Sundays at 3.30pm. The Saturday show is especially suitable for children aged 4 and above (€6.35).

Malahide Castle, the Fry Model Railway and Tara's Palace

Malahide, Co. Dublin ⓣ01/846 2184,
ⓦwww.malahidecastle.com. Mon–Sat 10am–5pm, also April–Sept Sun & public hols 10am–6pm. Oct–March Sun & public hols 10am–5pm. Adults €6.50, children €4, family €18.
Malahide began life in the late twelfth century as a tower house belonging to the Talbots. They retained possession for the next eight hundred years, modifying and expanding it from an easily defended stronghold into a comfortable, rambling home. Even so, in 1973, when the last of the line passed away, Malahide was still a castle, and it keeps the romantic look and feel of a fortress. Today it defends nothing more than an interesting collection of art and a jumble of architectural styles, pointed out during the guided tours. Look out for the small entranceway in the corner of the Great Hall known as "Puck's Door", named for a servant who reputedly slept through an attack by invaders and hung himself in shame, and whose ghost is believed to appear whenever changes threaten the castle.

The castle is also home to the Fry Model Railway (ⓣ01/846 3779, ⓦwww.visitdublin.com; April–Sept Mon–Sat 10am–1pm & 2–5pm; adults €6.50, children €4, family €18), the biggest in Ireland, covering almost 300 square yards. Its handmade models, some of which date back to the 1920s and 1930s, show the diversity of Ireland's transportation system. You won't just find plenty of trains from different periods of railway history (including the DART), but also a system centred upon the River Liffey replete with bridges and barges.

Your visit to Malahide should also include Tara's Palace (ⓣ01/846 3779; April–Sept Mon–Fri 10.45am–4.45pm; recommended minimum donation adults €2, children €1). Next to the Fry Model Railway, the palace is an astonishing, meticulously created doll's house, built to one-twelfth scale and inspired by genuine eighteenth-century mansions. Intricately furnished – there are real paintings hanging on its elegant walls and exquisite ornamentations grace its furniture and decor – it includes a chapel and a billiards room.

Also on display is a range of other antique doll's houses, including one owned by Oscar Wilde's mother, and a selection of toys dating back to as far as 1720.

National Gallery of Ireland

Merrion Square West, Dublin 2 ⓣ 01/661 5133, ⓦ www
.nationalgallery.ie. Mon–Sat 9.30am–5.30pm (Thurs until
8.30pm), Sun noon–5.30pm. Free.

The gallery's education department (ⓣ01/663 3505) mounts an extensive range of activities for children, including the Family Programme (Feb–June & Sept–Nov Sat 3pm; free) which offers opportunities for adults and children (aged 5–12) to explore art together through activities such as storytelling, craftwork and music. Additionally, there is a regular Children's Sunday Talk each week at 12.30pm, suitable for a similar age range, on a variety of art-related subjects, and special workshops in July for children aged 3–6 (Mon–Fri 11am–noon; €5 per class, €20 per week).

National Museum of Ireland – Archaeology and History

Kildare St, Dublin 2 ⓣ 01/677 7444, ⓦ www.museum.ie.
Tues–Sat 10am–5pm, Sun 2–5pm. Free.

Housing a wealth of prehistoric, Viking and medieval finds, as well as an Egyptian gallery, the National Museum's archaeological and historical collection offers an astonishing array of objects and artefacts, many of which will be of interest to children. It's Ór gallery is dedicated to prehistoric golden treasures, while the Prehistoric Ireland section incorporates a reconstruction of a Neolithic passage tomb, including decorated stones from Newgrange.

In the Viking Ireland gallery you'll discover the skeleton of a warrior alongside various rings and brooches, models of a Viking Dublin house and plenty of objects excavated from the city's Winetavern Street and Wood Quay. Medieval Ireland focuses on subjects as varied as weaponry and worship, as well as exhibits of games and a keg of bog butter. The small Egyptian room naturally includes mummies (always a winner), as well as hieroglyphic scripts and an astonishingly detailed model of a Nile boat. The Museum's Education and Outreach Department (ⓣ01/648 6453) runs a regular programme of events for children aged 7 upwards and activity sheets are available at the museum's reception.

National Museum of Ireland – Decorative Arts and History

Collins Barracks, Benburb St, Dublin 7 ⓣ 01/677 7444,
ⓦ www.museum.ie. Tues–Sat 10am–5pm, Sun 2–5pm. Free.

Housed in barracks dating from 1701, which surround the biggest drill square in Europe (capable of holding six regiments), the National Museum's Decorative Arts has some exhibits which may be of interest to older children (and activity sheets, suitable for 9- to 13-year-olds, are available at reception). The most intriguing selection is contained within the Curator's Choice gallery which includes eighteenth-century musical instruments as well as the cabinet given by Oliver Cromwell to his daughter as a wedding present. The "Out of Storage" gallery includes a striking seventeenth-century Japanese suit of armour and elsewhere you'll find intriguing clocks, scientific instruments, an impressive Victorian doll's house and "The Way We Wore" exhibition, tracing 250 years of Irish clothing. The museum runs a programme of events and activities for children of various ages once or twice a month (Sun 3–4pm) based around the exhibits.

National Museum of Ireland – Natural History Collection

Merrion St, Dublin 2 ⓣ01/677 7444, ⓦwww.museum.ie.
Tues–Sat 10am–5pm, Sun 2–5pm. Free.

Known to Dubliners as the "Dead Zoo", thanks to its vast collection of stuffed animals and birds and skeletons, the Natural History Museum always makes a great day out for the kids. The collection focuses on Irish wildlife on its ground floor including skeletons of the giant Irish deer, which became extinct around 9000 BC. The first floor houses the World Collection which includes all manner of simians, a rhinoceros and giraffes. Further upstairs, there's a stuffed dodo and a good vantage point to view the skeletons of two whales, once beached on Irish shores, which hang from the ceiling. Various activity sheets are provided to guide young minds through the galleries. The sheets are free at the ground-floor reception desk, where you'll also be able to pick up details of the Saturday Club (11am–noon) and Sunday activities sessions (3–4pm), together with the regularly changing programme of events they offer.

National Transport Museum

Heritage Depot, Howth Castle Demesne, Howth, Co. Dublin
ⓣ01/848 0831, ⓦwww.nationaltransportmuseum.org.
June–Aug Mon–Fri 10am–5pm; Sept–May Sat & Sun 2–5pm.
Adults €3, children €1.50, family €8.

Housed in a converted barn in the grounds of Howth Castle (not open to the public), the museum is home to buses and trams, fire engines and horse-drawn conveyances that add a vivid reality to children's view of the past. It's run by enthusiasts who proudly display photographs and transport memorabilia alongside the weird and wonderful vehicles.

National Wax Museum

Granby Row, Parnell Square, Dublin 1 ⓣ01/872 6340. Mon–Sat 10am–5.30pm, Sun noon–5.30pm. Adults €7, children €5, family €18.

Boasting more than three hundred exhibits, from Madonna to the Teletubbies, the Wax Museum is an enjoyable place to pass a couple of hours on a wet afternoon. Younger children will delight in the World of Fairytale and Fantasy and their quest for the magical lamp, while there are also plenty of tunnels to crawl through and a hall of mirrors. Older children will probably be absorbed by the Chamber of Horrors and, of course, there's always the opportunity to be photographed next to your favourite hero or heroine. For adults there's a re-creation of Da Vinci's *Last Supper*, literary figures, such as Joyce and Yeats; and a line-up of Irish prime ministers, featuring an incredibly sinister-looking Charles Haughey.

Newbridge House and Traditional Farm

Donabate, Co. Dublin ⓣ01/843 6534. April–Sept Tues–Sat 10am–5pm, Sun 2–6pm; Oct–March Sat & Sun 2–5pm. Adults €6.20, children €3.70, family €17.

While adults will relish a tour of this splendid Georgian mansion, dating from 1737, and admire its Rococo plasterwork and antique decor and furniture, the key attractions for children are the Museum of Curiosities and the Traditional Farm. The former includes such oddities as an arcane Kashmiri sari box and a clutch of ostrich eggs laid in Dundalk. The house's courtyard also includes a dairy, carpenter's shop and blacksmith's forge, all equipped with appropriate implements, while the farm is stocked with a variety of traditional animals.

North Bull Island

Accessed via Bull Bridge, off Clontarf Rd, Dublin 3, or the causeway leading from Watermill Rd, Dublin 5.

Apart from featuring the delights of the three-mile Dollymount Strand on its seaboard side, North Bull Island provides a temporary winter home to an enormous number of migratory birds, including one-sixth of the world's population of Brent geese. In summer, sea birds such as cormorants and oystercatchers are plainly visible while the island is also rich in wild flowers and inhabited by that increasing rarity, the Irish hare. You can learn more about the island and its residents at the Interpretive Centre by the beach at the end of the causeway (daily 10am–4.30pm; free).

Phoenix Park Visitor Centre

Phoenix Park, Dublin 8 ☏01/677 0095,
ⓦ www.heritageireland.ie. Jan to mid-March & Nov–Dec Sat &
Sun 10am–5pm; mid- to end March & Oct daily 10am–5.30pm;
April–Sept daily 10am–6pm. Adults €2.75, children €1.25,
family €7.

Spread over 1760 acres, Phoenix Park is the largest urban
park in Europe and would take several days to explore fully.
Home to Dublin Zoo (see p.15), the park also has its own
herd of three hundred deer which can sometimes be seen
roaming to the southwest of the Phoenix Memorial. The
park is dotted with cricket, football and hurling pitches and
polo fields, as well as including the Áras an Uachtarán (the
official residence of the Irish president) and the 92ft-high
stainless steel Papal Cross, situated on the spot where Pope
John Paul II celebrated Mass with a congregation of a million and a quarter people in September 1979. The park's visitor centre, near the northern Ashtown Gate, is a great place
to begin your visit; it has a child-oriented exhibition looking at the park's wildlife and illustrating the four and a half
thousand years of history represented by the Knockmaree
cist – an ancient grave found in the park in 1838 and reconstructed here.

Admission to the visitor centre also includes a tour of the
adjacent Ashtown Castle, a seventeenth-century tower
house, whose defensive features include a "murder hole" and
a staircase with a "trip step".

St Michan's Church

Church St, Dublin 7 ☏ 01/872 4154. March–Oct Mon–Fri
10am–12.30pm & 2–4.30pm, Sat 10am–12.45pm; Nov–March
Mon–Fri 12.30–3.30pm, Sat 10am–12.45pm. Adults €3.50, children €2.50.

Dating from 1095, St Michan's is the Northside's oldest surviving building, though much of it was rebuilt in 1685. The
vaults of its crypt have achieved renown thanks to the presence of a dozen bodies preserved by the dry environment
(the limestone walls absorb moisture), constant temperature
and methane generated by rotting vegetation beneath the
church. Thought to be between 300 and 700 years old, the
corpses include a woman reputed to have been be a nun, a
man missing a hand and an alleged Crusader – perfect
material for your bloodthirsty brood to dwell on. Other
vaults include the coffins of the Shears brothers, executed for
their part in the 1798 Rebellion, and the death-mask of the
Rebellion's leader, Wolfe Tone. The tours are superbly
informative and vary in duration according to the whim and
humour of the guide, but visitor numbers are strictly limited.

St Stephen's Green

Dublin 2. Mon–Sat 8am–dusk, Sun 10am–dusk. Free.

The centre of the most renowned and largest of Dublin's Georgian squares is occupied by a pleasant park whose gardens were originally laid out in 1880 for Lord Ardilaun (previously known as Sir Arthur Guinness) who donated the park to the people of Dublin. Featuring flower gardens, herbaceous borders, a bandstand occasionally used for outdoor concerts, and a lake full of waterfowl, the park makes an ideal spot for a summer picnic or a stroll.

Skerries Watermill and Windmills

Miller's Lane, Skerries, Co. Dublin ☎01/849 5208, ⓦhttp://indigo .ie/~skerries. Daily: April–Sept 10.30am–5.30pm; Oct–March 10.30am–4.30pm. Adults €5.50, children €4, family €12.

Set in the centre of Skerries Town Park, this complex features two windmills, a watermill complete with millraces and ponds alongside a field to provide grain for grinding. Visitors can see the machinery in action, learn about its history and have a go at grinding some corn. The tearooms here offer a broad range of musical entertainment, from traditional music to jazz, each Sunday lunchtime (call for details).

Trinity College Library and The Dublin Experience

College St, Dublin 2 ☎01/608 2320, ⓦwww.tcd.ie/library. Library: all year Mon–Sat 9.30am–5pm, also June–Sept Sun 9.30am–4.30pm & Oct–May Sun noon–4.30pm. Adults €7.50, children €6.50, family €15. The Dublin Experience: late May to early Oct daily 10am–5pm. Adults €4.20, children €3.50.

Ireland's oldest university, founded in 1592, is also the country's most popular tourist attraction. The reason is the Book of Kells, a fabulous ninth-century illustrated manuscript which forms the focus of the exhibition "Turning Darkness into Light" in the Old Library, though the book itself is displayed in the Treasury. The College's Arts and Social Sciences building houses the 45-minute audiovisual show, The Dublin Experience, which takes its audience through a thousand years of Dublin's history.

Viking Splash Tour on land and water

64–65 Patrick St, Dublin 8 ☎01/707 6000, ⓦwww .vikingsplashtours.com. Feb–May & Nov Tues–Sun; June–Oct daily tours every 30min 10am–5pm. Adults €15.50 except €17.50 weekends June & all days July & Aug; children €8.50 except €9.50 weekends June & all days July & Aug; family €48 except €52 weekends June & all days July & Aug.

For a truly different city tour, a trip on one of Viking

A walk around the Grand Canal

There are dozens of agreeable strolls to be had on the highways and byways of Dublin, but a walk along the banks of the Grand Canal is particularly pleasant because of the mixture of land and water it offers. The official Grand Canal Way comprises a three-and-a-half-mile loop commencing at the Waterways Visitor Centre before passing through leafy suburbs replete with pleasant Victorian architecture. South of Baggot Street Bridge, look out for the statue of the poet Patrick Kavanagh while, by Portobello Bridge, Portobello College originated as the Grand Canal Hotel in 1807, serving as a terminus for passenger barges which plied the canal. The walk ends at the junction of Dolphin Road and Spur Road, the latter leading to Kilmainham Gaol.

Splash's reconditioned World War II amphibious vehicles known as "Ducks" is essential. The tour sets off from Bull Alley and trundles around the city's sites and attractions before plunging into the waters of the Grand Canal Dock and taking a leisurely return trip along the River Liffey (don't panic, you won't get wet). Tours last an hour and a quarter and tickets may also be purchased at tourist centres.

Waterways Visitor Centre

Grand Canal Quay, Dublin 2 ☏ 01/677 7510, ⓦ www .waterwaysireland.org. June–Sept daily 9.30am–5.30pm; Oct–May Wed–Sun 12.30–5pm. Adults €2.50, children €1.20, family €6.35. The best way to approach the visitor centre is by taking a stroll along the banks of the Grand Canal which forms a loop around the inner Southside. The centre itself provides an entertaining account of Ireland's inland waterways, including samples of art and literature inspired by them, and various working models, such as a barge passing through a lock. If you're considering a holiday afloat, there's a video which recounts some of the most scenic attractions of the waterways and the centre also sells all manner of related guides, navigation charts and towpath trails.

Sports and activities

Cinemas

Savoy O'Connell St Upper, Dublin 1 ☏ 01/874 6000, ⓦ www.filminfo.net; **Screen Cinema** D'Olier St, Dublin 2 ☏ 01/672 5500, ⓦ www.filminfo.net; **UGC** Parnell St, Dublin 1 ☏ 01/872 8444, ⓦ www.ugc.ie.

Gaelic football and hurling

Major games, including the All-Ireland Finals in September, take place at Croke Park ℗ 01/836 3222.

Go-karting

Kylemore Indoor Karting Unit 1A, Kylemore Industrial Estate, Killeen Rd, Dublin 10 ℗ 01/626 1444, ⓦ www.kylemore-karting .com. Daily 11am–10pm. Ireland's largest indoor karting arena offers a choice of two almost 400yd-long tracks, each featuring hills, banked corners, flyovers and underpasses. Full instruction is given and helmets, gloves and race suits are provided. Ten minutes' practice on a single track costs €15, rising to €30 for 25 minutes, or you can try fifteen minutes on both tracks for €30. There's a special race for 9- to 14-year-olds (€20) each Sunday at 10am. A deposit of €100 is required when booking.

Horse racing

Leopardstown Racecourse Foxrock, Co. Dublin ℗ 01/289 3607, ⓦ www.leopardstown.com. Weekends throughout the year and Wednesday evenings in summer. There are also other race-courses close to Dublin, such as Punchestown, in Naas.

Leisureplex centres

Blanchardstown Centre, Blanchardstown, Dublin 15 ℗ 01/822 3030; Malahide Rd, Coolock, Dublin 17 ℗ 01/848 5722; Old Bray Rd, Stillorgan, Co. Dublin ℗ 01/288 1656; Village Green Centre, Tallaght, Dublin 24 ℗ 01/459 9411, ⓦ www.leisureplex.ie. Daily 12am–12pm. Each centre features the Zoo, an adventure play area, including a separate space for toddlers, ten-pin bowling and a live-action laser game. The Blanchardstown Centre also has dodgems.

Swimming

Markievicz Leisure Centre Townsend St, Dublin 2 ℗ 01/672 9121, ⓦ www.dublincity.ie. Mon–Thurs 7am–10pm, Fri 7am–9pm, Sat 9am–6pm, Sun 10am–4pm; adults €5, children €2.60 (under 2s free), family €9. Sessions last 45 minutes and commence on the hour. Open swimming sessions usually take place Mon–Fri, 9–11am & 2–4pm and Sat & Sun all day. Under 18s must be supervised by an adult.

National Aquatic Centre Snugborough Rd, Blanchardstown, Dublin 15 ℗ 01/646 4300, ⓦ www.nac.ie. Leisure pool July & Aug Mon–Fri 9am–9pm, Sat & Sun 9am–8pm; Sept–June Mon–Fri 2–8.45pm, Sat & Sun 9am–7.45pm; adults €12, children €10. As well as offering a competition pool for serious swimmers (call for times), the NAC's leisure pool includes a water roller coaster, surfing machine, wave and bubble pools, a pirate's ship and the Dark Hole Flume water slide. There's a special session for families (Sat 9–10am) and under 8s must be accompanied in the water by an adult at all times.

Theatres

The Abbey Theatre Abbey St Lower, Dublin 1 ☎ 01/878 7222, 🌐 www.abbeytheatre.ie; **Gaiety Theatre** King St South, Dublin 2 ☎ 01/677 1717, wwww.gaietytheatre.com; **Gate Theatre** 1 Cavendish Row, Parnell Square, Dublin 1 ☎ 01/874 4045, 🌐 www.gate-theatre.ie; **Olympia Theatre** 72 Dame St, Dublin 2 ☎ 01/677 1020.

Accommodation

Central Hotel 2–5 Exchequer St, Dublin 2 ☎ 01/679 7302, 🌐 www.centralhotel.ie. As its name suggests, this is in a prime central location.

Clifden Guesthouse 32 Gardiner Place, Dublin 1 ☎ 01/874 6364, 🌐 www.clifdenhouse.com. Comfortable, family-run establishment offering family accommodation.

Jurys Inn Christchurch Christchurch Place, Dublin 8 ☎ 01/454 0000, 🌐 www.bookajurysinn.com. Popular with families, thanks to its inclusive room rates. Rooms can accommodate two adults and two children.

Jacob's Inn 21–28 Talbot Place, Dublin 1 ☎ 01/855 5660, 🌐 www.dublinbackpacker.com. One of the best-equipped Dublin hostels, offering en-suite, four-bed rooms from €25 per person.

Leeson Inn Downtown 24 Leeson St Lower, Dublin 2 ☎ 01/662 2002, 🌐 www.leesoninndowntown.com. Elegant, four-storey Georgian townhouse with very competitive rates (children under 12 sharing with adults stay free).

Oliver St John Gogarty Apartments 18–21 Anglesea St, Temple Bar, Dublin 2 ☎ 01/671 1822, 🌐 www.gogartys.ie. Well worth considering for larger families wanting several days in Dublin, these self-catering apartments sleep four.

Places to eat

Beshoff's 14 Westmoreland St, Dublin 2 and 6 O'Connell St Upper, Dublin 1. Excellent sit-down fish and chips.

Botticelli 3 Temple Bar, Dublin 2. This place serves excellent pizza and has its own ice-cream parlour.

Café Kylemore St Stephen's Green Shopping Centre, Dublin 2 and Earl Street, Dublin 1. Child-friendly, self-service restaurants which offer a daily changing menu.

Captain America's 44 Grafton St, Dublin 2. A variety of steaks, chicken, burgers, seafood and vegetarian meals consumed within walls festooned with rock music memorabilia.

Hard Rock Café 12 Fleet St, Temple Bar, Dublin 2. Offers classic American food.

Elephant and Castle 18 Temple Bar, Dublin 2. Hugely popular upmarket burger restaurant also offering Cajun and Creole cuisine.

O'Shea's 23 Anglesea St, Temple Bar, Dublin 2. Popular family restaurant specializing in traditional Irish meals.

2

Wicklow and Kildare

K ildare lies just west of Dublin, and Wicklow just to the south of the city, making this part of Ireland very accessible indeed. The Dublin light rail network, the DART, goes out as far as Greystones on the Wicklow coast, and the main line continues to Arklow; most of the major tourist centres are served by buses. In Kildare, the railway more or less follows the major N4 and N7 roads and serves many of the sights.

Wicklow and Kildare offer a rural respite from the hectic capital. They have great opportunities for walking and cycling, as well as marvellous golden, sandy beaches for relaxing seaside days. More energetic families will love the wild, desolate Wicklow Mountains crossed by the 82-mile waymarked Wicklow Way, whilst in Kildare you can explore one of Ireland's major industries, racehorse-breeding, at the National Stud in Kildare town.

Information

Co. Wicklow: Check out Ⓦwww.wicklow.ie and Ⓦwww .wicklowtoday.com. Wicklow Tourism produces *The Wicklow Walking Guide*, sold in tourist offices, which are open all year at Arklow Ⓣ040/232 484; Athy Ⓣ598/633 07); Blessington Ⓣ045/865 850; Bray Ⓣ01/286 6796; Rathdrum Ⓣ040/446 262; and Wicklow Ⓣ040/469 117.

Co. Kildare: Ⓦwww.kildare.ie/touristguide/index.asp is recommended, as is the all-year tourist office in Kildare Ⓣ045/ 521 240.

Wicklow

Arklow Maritime Museum

St Mary's Rd, Arklow, Co. Wicklow ☎ 0402/32868. May–Sept
Mon–Sat 10am–1pm & 2–5pm; Oct–April Mon–Fri 10am–1pm &
2–5pm. Adults €7, children with an adult free.

A three-minute walk from the tourist office, the museum
traces Arklow's history from when the Vikings established
the town in the ninth century. The video presentation is
worth watching but the main attraction is the splendidly
varied collection which includes tools, models (with a ship
made from more than 10,000 matchsticks), a whale's tooth
and its eardrum.

Glenroe Open Farm

Ballygannon, Kilcoole, Co. Wicklow ☎ 01/287 2288,
ⓦ www.glenroefarm.com. March, Sept & Oct Sat–Sun
10am–5pm; April–Aug Mon–Fri 10am–5pm, Sat–Sun 10am–6pm.
Adults €4.25, children €3.50, family €14.

A charming stop just off the N11 main road about 20 miles south of Dublin, Glenroe offers a display of historic farm implements, and the chance to get close to farm animals such as donkeys, horses, goats, sheep, and pigs. You can also coo at the peacocks, rabbits, deer and other smaller fry on show. The coffee shop, picnic areas and outdoor playground will calm the over-excited before the return to base.

National Sea Life Centre

Strand Rd, Bray, Co. Wicklow ⓣ01/286 6939, ⓦwww.sealife.ie. March–Aug Mon–Fri 10am–6pm; Sat & Sun 10–6.30; Sept–Feb Mon–Fri 11am–5pm Sat & Sun 11am–6pm. Adults €8.50, children €5.50 (under 3s free), family €27.

The main attraction on the Bray seafront, this hi-tech, child-oriented aquarium successfully disguises serious educational material as entertainment for the whole family. It specializes in Irish marine life and can boast exhibits including sharks, octopus, a rock tunnel carved by a freshwater stream, and a touch pool with crabs and starfish. There's a subtle focus on conservation throughout the visit as children are quizzed using "magic" glasses to read coded questions and find answers on special scratchpads.

Powerscourt Estate and Waterfall

Enniskerry, Co. Wicklow ⓣ01/204 6000, ⓦwww.powerscourt.ie. House & gardens daily: March–Oct 9.30am–5.30pm; Nov–Feb 9.30am–dusk. Waterfall daily: summer 9.30am–7pm; winter 10.30am–dusk. House and garden: adults €8 summer/€6.50 winter, children €4.50 summer/€4.10 winter, under 5s free. Waterfall: adults €4, children over 5 €3.

This partly restored eighteenth-century Palladian mansion some twelve miles south of Dublin off the N11 is one of Ireland's grandest estates, with a Japanese garden, walled garden and other magnificent formal expanses with a backdrop of the Wicklow hills.

The kids will enjoy climbing the Pepper Pot Tower and the great views it offers, and some of them will relish the pet cemetery. The house itself is less of a must-see as it now functions mainly as a shopping centre, but the terraced café and picnic area make good resting points. The playground nearby is worth looking in on if there's excess energy to burn off before the four-mile signposted walk through the estate.

A three-mile drive following signs along the road takes you to the highest waterfall in Ireland (daily: summer 9.30am–7pm; winter 10.30am–dusk; €3.50), where the quiet River Dargle turns suddenly angry before plunging some 400ft into the valley below. Mother Nature's other local attractions are highlighted along the nature trail that runs around the base of the fall; at less than a mile, it makes a suitably low-stress end to an exciting visit.

Clara Lara Fun Park

Vale of Clara, Rathdrum, Co. Wicklow ☏ 0404/46161. May–Aug 10am–6pm. Adults €7, children €3 (under 4s free), additional charges for some activities.

This outdoor adventure park by the Avonmore River promises a feast of water-based fun and mini golf. Try your hand at go-karting, hill-walking, rafting or canoeing while the rest of the family explores the treehouses, wooden playgrounds, pirate galleon and water slides. Summer visits are great for barbecues and picnics, and Santa Claus stops by in December; phone for details.

Avondale House and Forest Park

Rathdrum, Co. Wicklow ☏ 0404/46111, ⓦ www.coillte.ie/tourism_and_recreation-2003 /avondale_home_parnell.htm. Daily mid-March to Oct 11am–6pm. House: adults €5.50, family €16.

This splendid Georgian house, built in 1777, has been restored to the decor of circa 1850. Now a museum to political leader Charles Stewart Parnell (1846–91), it is set in magnificent forested grounds. Children will enjoy romping up and down the nature trails, where badgers, otters and ninety species of birds and other wildlife may be spotted, and will adore the residents of the deer pen. There's also a picnic area, play area, a gift shop and café.

Wicklow Historic Gaol

Kilmartin Hill, Wicklow Town ☏ 0404/61599, ⓦ www .wicklowhistoricgaol.com. Daily mid-March to Oct 10am–6pm, tours every 10 min. Adults €6.80, children €3.95, family with up to three children €18.20.

Times were hard for criminals in the eighteenth century. This gaol was built in 1702 with more than 400 inmates sharing the 42 cells: they were fed once every four days and allowed fifteen minutes' exercise in the prison yard per month. The costumed guides offer a lively re-creation of the grim prison conditions, and make a powerful impression on children, who soon learn that in the eighteenth and nineteenth centuries they would have been welcomed to stay just as readily as adults. Tours last 60–90 minutes and focus on the role the gaol played after the 1798 Rebellion and on the lives of those sent from here to the colonies.

Kildare

Larchill Arcadian Garden

Kilcock, Co. Kildare ☎ 01/628 7354. May & Sept Sat & Sun
noon–6pm; June–Aug noon–6pm. Adults €7, children €5 (under
4s free), family €25.

On the Dunshaughlin Road, signposted off the N4 main
road near Maynooth, this 63-acre parkland contains Europe's
only surviving ornamental farm – the precursor to the modern landscape garden – and is a feast of decorative buildings, statuary, water features and a lake with castle follies. Of
more immediate interest to younger members of the family
are nature trails, a splendid wooden adventure trail, and
indoor play area. There's a puppet theatre, magic shows on
Saturdays, a maze in summer, a walled garden with peacocks,
and animals galore on the farm – including llamas. A ghost
haunts the cockleshell-covered tower, and there is also a pet
corner, sandpit, playground with old-fashioned games, and a
café.

Irish National Stud

Kildare town ☎ 045/521617, ⓦ www.irish-national-stud.ie. Daily
mid–Feb to mid–Nov 9.30am–6pm; guided tours on the hour
from 11am. Adults €9, children €4.50, family €20.

Those not yet old enough to invest speculatively on the rela-
tive speed of the animals living here will still find a visit to
the National Stud fascinating. This is the heart of the Irish
racing world, and a trip to the stud, on the Tully Estate on
the south side of Kildare, signposted from the town centre, is
the best way to get close to the breeding, training and atten-
tion to detail that makes Irish horses so supremely valuable.
As well as the thoroughbreds themselves, you'll get to see
stallion boxes, a museum and a spotlessly clean complex of
white buildings set amongst green lawns and overshadowed
by the bleak ruins of the Black Abbey. Don't miss the ornate
Japanese Garden and tranquil St Fiachra's Garden, a beautiful
place of lakes and monastic cells.

Lullymore Heritage and Discovery Park

Lullymore, Co. Kildare ☎ 045/870238
ⓦ www.kildare.ie/tourism/sites/lullymore. Easter–Oct Mon–Fri
9am–6pm, Sat & Sun noon–6pm; Nov–March Mon–Fri
9am–4.30pm. €3.50, family €8.

Set in wooded parkland in the Bog of Allen, the
woodland/bog walkways and reconstructions of a Mesolithic
campsite with a Neolithic dwelling nearby are fascinating.

Children will also enjoy the road train rides, a trip to the little fairy bower, a visit to the café and working off any excess steam at Fionn MacCumhaill's Adventure Park (named after a mythological hero whose reputed birthplace, the Hill of Allen, overlooks the site) – where the attractions include a castle, climbing frames, swings, slides, sand pits, fireman's poles and crazy golf. Also featured is the Indoor Play Centre, based on a forest theme (adults €9, children €8, family €25).

Maynooth Castle

Maynooth, Co. Kildare ☎ 01/628 6744,
Ⓦ www.heritageireland.ie. June–Sept Mon–Fri 10am–6pm, Sat & Sun 1–6pm; Oct Sun 1–5pm. Free, 45min guided tours €1.90. Heritage Card.

A thirteenth-century ruin good for scrambling around and swashbuckling, this castle contains an exhibition on the occasionally bloodthirsty history of the Fitzgeralds, the Anglo-Norman dynasty that owned it. Maynooth Castle sits next to the entrance to St Patrick's College, and was one of the family's main strongholds. A massive stone eminence, it kept Kildare – in fact, most of the rest of Ireland – under Fitzgerald control until the arrival of the Tudors.

Millennium Maze, Prosperous

Ballinafagh Farm, Prosperous, Co. Kildare ☎ 045/868151,
Ⓦ www.themillenniummaze.com. Daily May–Sept noon–6pm. Adults €6, children €4, family €20.

This 6ft-high hedge maze was grown on Ballinafagh Farm to mark the millennium. In the shape of a St Brigid's Cross, it has over one and a half miles of paths. There's also an unenclosed, paved maze, which is a thoughtful added attraction for younger children, who will appreciate the crazy golf course, sand pit and pets' corner (with ducks, sheep, hens and rabbits) too. The café and picnic area make a good base for those too tired to explore.

Straffan Butterfly Farm

Ovidstown, Straffan, Co. Kildare ☎ 01/627 1109, Ⓦ www .straffanbutterflyfarm.com. Daily May–Aug noon–5.30pm. Adults €6, children €4, family €16.

Three miles southwest of Celbridge (signposted from Kill), this farm has a tropical greenhouse where butterflies flutter by freely, while glass tanks safely keep the fiercer-looking inmates – including an assortment of reptiles, stick insects, bird-eating spiders, scorpions and tarantulas – away from the visitors. Those so inclined can satisfy their creepy-crawly passion, while the butterflies make it a fun and unforgettable experience for all visitors.

Straffan Steam Museum

Straffan, Co. Kildare ☏01/627 3155, ⓦwww.steam-museum.ie.
May & Sept by arrangement in advance; June–Aug Wed–Sun
2–6pm. Adults €7.50, children €5, family €20.

Signposted from the N7 road at Kill village, Lodge Park
Heritage Centre's Steam Museum is housed in a Victorian
church. A rose-tinted look back to the good old days of the
industrial revolution, it contains miniature models of steam
trains, locomotives dating from the eighteenth century and
four working steam engines burbling away quietly. The early
August holiday weekend brings a steam rally, with even
more engines on show, and narrow-gauge railway rides set
up in the grounds. Refuge from all this engineering may be
found in the museum teahouse or in the eighteenth-century
walled garden (adults €4, children €3).

Sports and activities

Bicycle rental

Footfalls Trooperstown, Roundwood, Co. Wicklow
☏0404/45152, ⓦwww.walkinghikingireland.com; **Johnny
Price's Garage** Main St, Roundwood, Co. Wicklow,☏01/281
8128; **Hillcrest Hire**, Main St, Blessington, Co. Wicklow
☏045/865066.

Cinema

Ormonde Cinema Upper Main St, Arklow; **Cineplex** Bray, Co.
Wicklow ☏01/286 8686; **Screen by the Sea** Victoria Rd,
Greystones, Co. Wicklow ☏01/287 1143.

Cycling tours

Cycling Safaris Belfield Bike Shop, University College Dublin
☏01/260 0749, ⓦwww.cyclingsafaris.com. Offers seven-day
self-led tours of Wicklow.

Fishing

Viking Tackle 79 Castle St, Bray, Co. Wicklow ☏01/286 9215.
Pick up angling permits for the Dargle River as well as advice.
Daily permits €10.

Motor racing

Mondello Park Co. Kildare ☏045/860200, ⓦ www
.mondellopark.com. Check for details, although there'll be something exciting going on most weekends from March to October.

Horse riding

Co. Wicklow: **Brennanstown Riding School** Hollybrook, Kilmacanogue, Bray ⓣ 01/286 3778; **Broomfield Riding School** Broomfield, Tinahely ⓣ 0402/38117; **Devil's Glen Holiday and Equestrian Village** Ashford ⓣ 0404/40637, Ⓦ www.devilsglen.ie; **Paulbeg Riding School** Shillelagh ⓣ 055/29100.

Co. Kildare: **Abbeylands Equestrian Centre** Clane, ⓣ 045/868188; **Kill International Equestrian Centre** Kill ⓣ 045/877208.

Water sports and adventure sports

Blessington Adventure Centre Blessington, Co. Wicklow ⓣ 045/865092. Choose between sailing, canoeing, windsurfing, kayaking, tennis, pony trekking, riding and archery.

The National Mountain and Whitewater Centre Devil's Glen Forest, Ashford, Co. Wicklow ⓣ 0404/40169, Ⓦ www.tiglin.com. Weekend courses in mountaineering, rock climbing and whitewater kayaking.

Accommodation

Glendaloch International Hostel Co. Wicklow; ⓣ 0404/45342. Private family rooms and dorms, bike rental.

Kildare Hotel and Country Club Straffan, Co. Kildare ⓣ 01/601 7200, Ⓦ www.kclub.ie. Luxury hotel with indoor swimming pool, tennis, squash, gym, babysitting.

Old Presbytery Hostel Rathdrum, Co. Wicklow ⓣ 0404/46930. Comfortable accommodation including dorms and private family rooms.

Tynte House Dunlavin, Co. Wicklow ⓣ 045/401561. Good one- to five-bed self-catering apartments and cottages. It's ideal for families, having a grassy play area, treehouse, games room with table tennis and pool.

Roundwood Caravan and Camping Park Roundwood, Co. Wicklow ⓣ 01/281 8163, Ⓦ www.dublinwicklowcamping.com. May to mid-Sept. Facilities include a shop, restaurant and play areas.

Wicklow Bay Hostel Wicklow Town, Co. Wicklow ⓣ 0404/69213, Ⓦ www.wicklowbayhostel.com; Feb–Nov. Has dorms, four-bed and twin rooms ideal for budget-conscious families.

Places to eat

The Bakery Restaurant Church St, off Fitzwilliam Square, Wicklow town ☎0404/66770. A good variety of child-friendly options including ciabatta sandwiches, panini, salads, seafood, pork and rice dishes, all in a pleasant, bistro-style setting.

Kristianna's Bistro The Square, Kildare town ☎045/522985. Specializes in seafood; children can have half-portions.

Poppies Country Kitchen Enniskerry, Co. Wicklow ☎01/282 8869. Home-made lunches (shepherd's pie, quiche, chicken and chips and lasagne, for example), salads, cakes, puddings and teas, open until 6.30pm in summer. Half-portions are available.

Strawberry Tree Restaurant *Brooklodge Hotel*, Macreddin village, Co. Wicklow ☎0402/36444. Try this restaurant for a top-notch meal made exclusively from organic, free-range and wild ingredients.

The Wicklow Heather Laragh, Co. Wicklow ☎0404/45157. A popular inn with a moderately priced family restaurant offering steaks, chops and stews.

3

Laois and Offaly

Comparatively few families holiday in Laois (pronounced "leash") and Offaly, and perhaps that's part of their charm. The landscape of this region between Dublin and the Shannon is seldom breathtaking, yet

there are some beautiful areas, notably around the signposted Slieve Bloom Way, 52km/32 miles of tracks through the bog, moorland and pine forest around the Slieve Bloom Mountains.

The main N7 trunk road and main rail line to Limerick cut through the centre of Laois, while the N52 main road straddles Tullamore, the centre of Offaly, and the rail and road hub for the county. Buses from all the major towns pass through Portlaoise, and there are daily services from Dublin to Portumna, and from Cork to Athlone.

Laois

The Abbey Sense Garden

Main St, Abbeyleix, Co. Laois ⊤0502/31325. May–Sept daylight hours, free.

The walks through the tranquil sensory gardens of the Brigidine Dove House Convent lead you round the flowerbeds designed to stimulate your senses of vision, smell, touch, taste and sound; on fine days they can give off a combination of smells more potent than a department store perfume counter.

Heywood House Gardens

Ballinakill, Co. Laois ⊤0502/33563, ⓦwww.heritageireland.ie. Daily dawn to dusk. Free. Phone ahead for guided tours.

Little more than a couple of miles southeast of Abbeyleix, children can let off steam on the lawns of these formal gardens. There are nice little touches, such as the stone turtles by the fountain.

Workhouse and Agricultural Museum

Donaghmore, Portlaoise, Co. Laois ⊤0505/46212. May–Sept Mon–Fri 10am–5pm.

A visit here gives some idea of the grimmer aspects of the county's history following the Great Famine of 1845–49. The moving, stimulating, story that unfolds in this harsh building, which served as the parish workhouse between 1853 and 1886, highlights the extent of rural poverty in the nineteenth century. The overwhelming size of the establishment indicates the sheer scale of the problem. Families were frequently broken up on admission and on average two of the eight hundred inmates died each week (more ghoulish visitors might be interested to know that they were buried in a mass grave at the back of the building).

Stradbally Steam Museum

The Green, Stradbally, Co. Laois ☎ 0502/25444, ⓦ www
.irishsteam.ie. Adults €3, children over 4 €1.
As well as showing a variety of weird and wonderful mechanical exhibits such as ancient fire engines, steam-driven tractors and massive steamrollers, each August the museum hosts the Irish Steam Preservation Society steam-engine rally, which attracts vintage cars too. Call the Portlaoise tourist office for more details.

Stradbally is also home to a Guinness Brewery steam locomotive of 1895 that runs up to Dublin six times each year. The railway is open 2.30–5pm bank holiday weekends and Sundays and Mondays from Easter to October, as well as on selected other days in connection with local events; call for details.

Offaly

Birr Castle and Historic Science Centre

Birr, Co. Offaly ☎ 0509/20336, ⓦ www.birrcastle.com. Daily:
March–Oct 9am–6pm; Nov–Feb 10am–4pm. Adults €9, children
€5, family €24.
Much of the castle is still used as a family home and so remains closed, but the grounds, with their wild-flower meadows, artificial lake and a river spanned by a suspension bridge, are beautiful, and open to visitors year-round. They're the scene of many special events for children including Easter-egg hunts, puppet shows, country fairs, Hallowe'en parties and Santa visits. The Historic Science Centre is now home to a collection of optical equipment that culminates with the 72-inch Great Telescope, built during the 1840s by the Earl of Rosse, and the largest in the world at that time.

Transport and Heritage Museum

Clonmacnoise, Co. Offaly ☎ 090/643 0106. Daily May–Sept
10am–5.30pm. Adults €4, children €3.

This small museum 5 miles east of town, just off the main N62 Athlone-Roscrea road, somehow manages to cram in one thousand exhibits. The collection boasts vintage cars, agricultural vehicles, a threshing mill and other farm machinery, plus a cable car and a very varied collection of bygones including – for no obvious reason – a high number of typewriters and butter churns.

Clonmacnoise

Shannonbridge, Co. Offaly ℡090/967 4195, Ⓦwww .heritageireland.ie. Daily: Nov to mid-March 10am–5.30pm; mid-March to mid-May 10am–6pm; mid-May to Aug 9am–7pm; Sept & Oct 10am–6pm. Adults €5, children €2, family €11.

Clonmacnoise stands out even among the other Celtic sites crowding the banks of the Shannon, as Ireland's most important early Christian centre. Located 14 miles from Athlone and signposted from the main N62 road, the monastic complex founded here in 548 is now little more than a clutch of ancient ruins which barely show themselves above the open ground, dwarfed by a new visitor centre and crowds that come here. But it was once a huge and important centre of worship and learning. Having hidden away from the Vikings and repulsed the Normans, the monastery finally gave way to the English in 1552 and never recovered. Evening visits avoid most of the hubbub and permit quiet reflection on what was a great cauldron of craftsmanship, a royal city and final resting place for the kings of Ireland. Children will have fun charging between the ruined cathedral, the eight ten- to thirteenth-century churches and the two round towers, whilst the adults check out the audiovisual show and café.

Clonmacnoise and West Offaly Railway

Bord na Mona/The Irish Peat Board, Blackwater Works, Shannonbridge, Co. Offaly ℡090/967 4450, Ⓦwww.bnm.ie. April–Oct daily 10am–5pm; Nov–March by request only. Adults €5, children €4.50, family €20.

This narrow-gauge railway takes you on a 45-minute, 5.5-mile circular guided tour around Blackwater Bog, a 12,000-year-old section of preserved peatlands. Tours leave on the hour after you've seen a video of the history of the bog and its flora and fauna.

Charleville Forest Castle

Tullamore, Co. Offaly ℡0506/21279. April–May, Sat & Sun 2–5pm; June–Sept Wed–Sun 11am–4pm; Oct–March by appointment. Minimum €15 for tour for up to three people, then €5 per adult, children 12–18 €4, children 6–11 €4, under 6s free.

You could be forgiven for believing you've been spirited away into a horror film when you set eyes upon this striking limestone Georgian Gothic pile built in 1779. A classic "mad-scientist" mansion, with towers, spires and turrets, the house also has secret passageways and spooky dungeons with wonderful shaded walks and a grotto on the outside. About ten minutes' walk from the centre of Tullamore, it's just off the Birr road out of town (N52).

Sports and activities

Adventure and activity centres

Birr Outdoor Education Centre Roscrea Rd, Birr, Co. Offaly ☏ 0509/20029. The centre runs courses in kayaking, windsurfing, rock climbing and so on, and doubles as the Slieve Bloom Interpretive Centre, with information on the region.

Bicycle rental

K. Donegan Main St, Banagher, Co. Offaly ☏ 0509/51178; **Laurel Lodge** Garrymore, Shannonbridge, Co. Offaly ☏ 090/9674189; **Racha House** Shannonbridge, Co. Offaly ☏ 090/9674249.

Boat rental

Laurel Lodge Garrymore, Shannonbridge, Co. Offaly ☏ 090/967 4189. A B&B that also rents out a boat on the Shannon for four people, €50 per day, free to residents.
Shannon Adventure Canoeing Holidays The Marina, Banagher, Co. Offaly ☏ 0509/51411. Rent a canoe, €40 per day or €15 per first hour, €10 each hour thereafter.
Rachra House Shannonbridge, Co. Offaly ☏ 090/967 4249. A B&B that also rents out boats.

Bowling

Bowls Stadium Heritage Golf and Country Club, Portlaoise, Co. Laois ☏ 0502/42320; **Roll N' Bowl** Bowling and children's adventure centre, Clonminan Industrial Estate, Portlaoise, Co. Laois ☏ 0502/70005.

Cinemas

Storm Cinema Portlaiose, Co. Laois ☏ 050/ 262626.

Accommodation

The Glebe Caravan and Camping Park Clonfanlough, Co. Offaly ℡0902/30277. Open Easter–Oct in a tranquil spot near Clonmacnoise.

Preston House Main St, Abbeyleix, Co. Laois ℡0502/31432. A comfortable base for the handful of family-friendly attractions nearby. Good-quality rooms.

Roundwood House Mountrath, Co. Laois ℡0502/32120. As well as a friendly welcome in a great base for exploring the Slieve Bloom Mountains, *Roundwood* offers beautiful parkland containing goats, cows, donkeys, woodland walks and a swing.

Places to eat

Anatolia Harbour St, Tullamore, Co. Offaly ℡0506/23669; closed lunch Sat, dinner Fri & Sat. Mixed international menu; for an exotic change – most kids love the Turkish food on offer.

Kingfisher Indian Restaurant Main St, Portlaoise, Co. Laois ℡0502/62500. A well-established restaurant, particularly accommodating to families.

Preston House Restaurant Main St, Abbeyleix, Co. Laois ℡0502/31432; closed Mon. Good home cooking including scones and home-made preserves and breads, and great vegetarian dishes.

The Vine House Restaurant and Music Bar Banagher, Co. Offaly ℡0509/51463. Restaurant closed Nov–Feb. With a courtyard garden. Many dishes are around €10, with kids' half-portions half-price. Children's menu (€6.50) includes usual staples such as burgers, chicken nuggets and pasta.

4

Meath, Westmeath and Longford

The eastern counties extending from the coast north of Dublin into the heart of the country are perfect for families looking for a rural break. Very different from the west of the country, Meath, Westmeath and Longford are not rich in traditional attractions, although County Meath boasts the largest Norman fortress in Ireland at Trim. Westmeath's jewels are its lakes. The River Shannon roughly shapes the western border of County Longford, another region of extensive farmland. Its waterways attract families for boating and other water-based activities.

As for access, a main railway line skirts southern Meath, branching off at Mullingar in the centre of Westmeath to both Longford town and Athlone, which as the main transport hub of the area has buses departing for many main towns around the country. The N1, N2, N3, N4 and N6 trunk roads branch out from Dublin like the fingers of a hand, between them covering most areas of the three counties.

Meath

Funtasia

Bettystown, Co. Meath ☏041/982 8301.
This is a state-of-the-art entertainment centre with a heap of attractions to amuse the whole family, and all under cover. There's a top-notch bowling alley and fully equipped pool and snooker rooms for the older members of the family, while younger children will have a great time in the multi-level play area and disco. Funtasia also has its own indoor fairground with dodgems and other rides, fast food and a licensed restaurant.

Brú na Boinne

Donore, Co. Meath ☏041/988 0300, ⓦwww.heritageireland.ie.
Daily June to mid-Sept 9am–7pm; Oct–May 9.30am–5pm.
Combined Newgrange & Knowth tickets: adults €9.50, children €4.50, family €24.50; Newgrange site only: adults €5.50, children €2.75, family €13.75; Knowth site only: adults €4.25, children €1.50, family €10.50; visitor centre: adults €2.75, children €1.50, family €7.
Brú na Boinne, located between Slane and Drogheda on the River Boyne, is one of the most atmospheric ancient sites in the country, guaranteed to enthral young minds. A series of forty or so windswept prehistoric monuments more than five thousand years old, they predate the Pyramids and Stonehenge and are unmatched anywhere in Europe.

things not to miss

You'll never manage to see everything the country has to offer in a single trip – and we don't suggest you try. But we've made a selection of activities and attractions that we think represents the best the country has to offer families, to help you get the best out of your trip.

01 Dingle Peninsula Tranquil beauty a speciality.

FÁILTE IRELAND

02 Open farms Open farms offer unforgettable days of peace and quiet.

FÁILTE IRELAND

03 The Burren Unique, and outstandingly beautiful.

04 Kissing the Blarney Stone
And for evermore you'll have the gift of the gab.

05 Lough Erne
A perfect spot for a variety of watersports.

06 The open road
Take to the highways in a traditional gypsy caravan, and the whole country lies at your feet.

FÁILTE IRELAND

07 **Festivals and fairs** Ireland boasts a range of fairs and festivals.

TOURISM IRELAND

08 **A visit to the pub** A drink, a chat, a quiet sit down to watch the world pass by.

COLLECTIONS/ALAN LE GARSMEUR

09 **The Giant's Causeway** Arguably the world's oldest adventure playground.

10 Pony trekking

Whether it's along the wild coastline or through dreamy rural valleys, there's no better way to appreciate the country.

11 Galway Arts Festival

Fun for all the family.

CORBIS/ALEN MACWEENEY

12 **Fishing** Ireland's national sport

13 Connemara countryside The hills and valleys stretch out into the distance, without end.

FAILTE IRELAND

14 Sailing Ireland's a fantastic place to take your family afloat.

FAILTE IRELAND

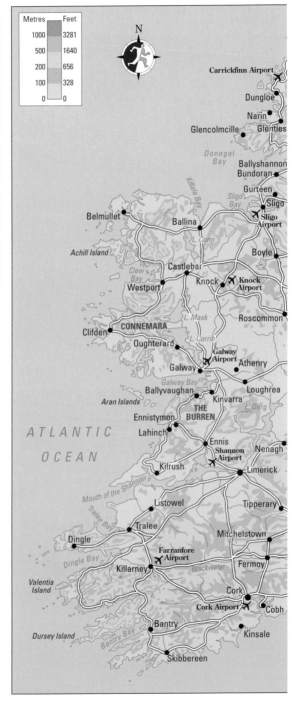

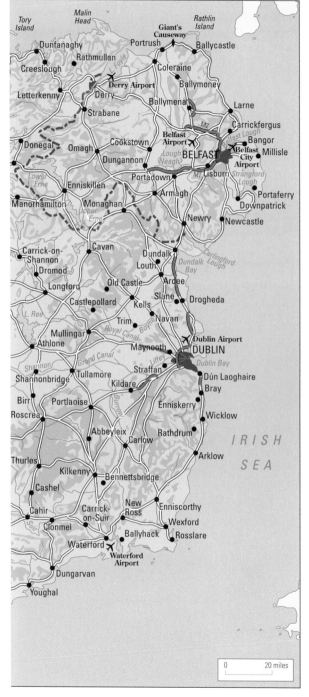

15 Traditional music
A skilled player is guaranteed an appreciative audience.

TOURISM IRELAND

16 Boat trips
Explore Ireland's coastline from the sea.

FÁILTE IRELAND

FÁILTE IRELAND

17 Hurling Nothing matches the thrills of a hurling match.

VIKING SPLASH TOURS

18 Viking Splash Tours Take home memories of this very different way to see the sights of Dublin.

WERNER FORMAN ARCHIVES

19 The Golden Ship Don't miss the Viking treasures of the National Museum.

FÁILTE IRELAND

20 **Cliffs of Moher** Clare's most majestic natural attraction.

THE IRISH IMAGE COLLECTION

21 **Kilmainham Gaol** Now restored and reopened as a visitor attraction.

22 St Patrick's Day Parade
The green face paint is optional, but having fun is not.

FÁILTE IRELAND

23 Galway City
A lovely old city that's full of surprises.

FÁILTE IRELAND

FÁILTE IRELAND

24 **The Skelligs** One of Ireland's classic seascapes – and most spectacular ferry destinations.

TOURISM IRELAND

25 **Grub! And plenty of it!** Tuck into some traditional Irish baking.

COLLECTIONS/ALAIN LE GARSMEUR

26 **Ulster Folk and Transport Museum** One of the thirty or so typical buildings making up the "museum village".

27 Carrick-a-rede rope bridge Just keep telling yourself that it's perfectly safe, and try not to look down.

28 Newgrange One of the most important stone age sites in Europe.

COLLECTIONS/PHIL THOMAS

29 **Fungi the dolphin** Famous for entertaining visitors to Dingle, he's a fun guy to be around

FÁILTE IRELAND

30 **Walking** Take the kids into the great outdoors.

The East Coast and Midlands Tourism HQ is in Mullingar (℡044/48650) and its website, covering all three counties, is ⓦ www.eastcoastmidlandstourism.ie. Further information is available for Meath from ⓦ www.meathtourism.ie, and for Longford from the Midlands East Tourism Office (℡044/48761).

Tourist offices are at Navan ℡046/9073426; Trim ℡046/9437111; and Longford ℡043/46566.

The most important are the three passage graves named Newgrange, Dowth and Knowth – high round mounds raised over stone burial chambers. The scale of the constructions is stunning: Newgrange, the largest of the trio, looms 36ft tall and is vast, covering more than an acre with a diameter of 260ft. An immense number of giant boulders were somehow heaved up to the site – with one major quartz element coming all the way from the mountains at Wicklow – to be tamped down with what has been estimated as more than a million sacks of smaller stones. Its distinguishing feature is a slitted rock at the entrance, through which a beam of light from the rising sun on the day of the winter solstice enters to illuminate the interior of the tomb. A sixty-foot passage leads to the burial chamber.

Newgrange is Ireland's most famous prehistoric monument, classed as a World Heritage Site by UNESCO. However, Knowth has only recently opened to the public, and even now just part of the complex may be visited and Dowth remains closed to visitors while excavations continue. The visitor centre has a café, along with viewing areas and interpretive displays that make it the best starting-point for seeing the monuments.

Be Irish for a Day!

Causey Farm, Girley, Fordstown, Navan, Co. Meath ℡046/943 4135, ⓦ www.causeyexperience.com. Open by appointment for groups, check for availability for individuals. Costs vary.

Don't be put off by the name – this is a great way to spend a day. Something out of the ordinary round of tourist fodder, Causey Farm encourages dirty hands and gently exhausting activities such as treasure hunts, nature trails and modelling with clay. Children can learn how to cut turf, have a bash at hurling, experiment with baking bread, and even dance a jig. Other attractions include working a sheepdog and milking a cow.

Grove Garden and Tropical Bird Sanctuary

Kells, Co. Meath ☏ 046/9434276. May–Sept daily 10am–6pm;
Mid-Feb to end April Sat & Sun 10am–6pm. Adults €6, children
€3, family €20.

A very pleasant day out can be had at the Grove, where the
tranquil formal gardens, which boast some four hundred different roses, give way first to the raucous tropical bird garden, where exotic and rare breeds of birds are housed in
purpose-built aviaries, and then to a mini-zoo that's home to
camels, monkeys and racoons.

Athlumney Castle

Convent Rd, Navan, Co. Meath. No telephone; open to visitors;
pick up the keys from Loreto Convent, just before you come to
the castle.

Worth the walk of a mile or so from Navan centre, past the
bridge and following the signs, this four-storeyed tower
house, which dates from the mid-fifteenth century, is now in
ruins, providing much excitement. There are four floors and
turrets to explore, with a secret chamber hidden away down
the stairs in the wall on the first floor.

Loughcrew Gardens

3 miles south of Oldcastle, Co. Meath ☏ 049/854 1922,
ⓦ www.loughcrew.com. Mid-March to Sept 12.30–5pm; Oct to
mid-March Sun & bank hols 1-4pm. Adults €6, children €3.50,
family €18.

Loughcrew's carefully restored gardens include a woodland
maze, a watermill cascade and a fairy grotto. The signposted
nature and history trails will captivate most younger visitors,
while the playground ought to enthral the rest. There's a café
for teas, coffees and light meals, or a fine country pub – *The
Fincourt* – up in the village, where seafood is a speciality.

Slane Castle

Slane, Co. Meath ☏ 041/9884400, ⓦ www.slanecastle.ie. May 2
to Aug 1 Mon–Thurs & Sun noon–5pm. Adults €7, children €5,
family €20.

Tours

Several tours are available from Dublin to Meath's main sites
from operators that include Bus Éireann (☏ 01/836 6111,
ⓦ www.buseireann.ie), Gray Line (☏ 01/676 5377, ⓦ www
.grayline.com) and the very child-friendly Over the Top Tours
(☏ 01/838 6128, ⓦ www.overthetoptours.com). The tourist
offices in Dublin can book tickets in advance.

Kids love castles, and Slane – set in a 1500-acre estate laid out by Capability Brown – is a great example. It dates from 1785 – although what you see today is mostly the result of restoration and renovation, following an extensive fire in 1992. The castle boasts an impressive set of battlements and turrets, never intended for real defence, which today has little to keep at bay except the rock fans who engulf the grounds once a year for enormous open-air gigs. Tours take in one of the finest art collections in the country, the main hall, King's Room and ballroom. To finish the visit there's a fine-looking mill across the main road outside the castle, and from Slane village you can walk up the Hill of Slane and scrabble around on the ruined Friary Church. Older children can climb the steep steps of its tower for a great view of the eastern counties.

Newgrange Farm

Slane, Co. Meath Ⓣ041/982 4119, Ⓦwww.newgrangefarm.com. Daily May–Aug 10am–5pm. €6 per person, €15 family of three, €5 per person thereafter.

Newgrange is a fun farm, and a delightful place to visit. Feed the ducks, bottle-feed the baby lambs and kid goats (if you visit in spring), see horseshoeing and working sheepdogs. At 3pm on Sundays there's a sheep derby, where hapless fleeced runners piloted by teddy-bear jockeys hurtle around a track, an event that manages to be both exciting and hilarious at the same time.

Trim Castle

Trim, Co. Meath Ⓣ046/943 8619, Ⓦwww.heritageireland.ie. Daily May–Oct 10am–6pm. Adults €3.50, children €1.25, family €8.25 including 45min guided tour of the keep, from 10.15am and then every 30min; adults €1.50, children €0.75, family €4.25 excluding the keep. Heritage Card.

Trim was used as a location for Mel Gibson's 1995 film *Braveheart*, and is the biggest and most obvious attraction in town, although there are numerous other medieval remains in the vicinity. The largest Anglo-Norman castle in Ireland, dating back to 1173, it dominates the little town even today. Get there early for the tour of the keep as it is very popular. It is safe but a steep climb, and unsuitable for small children.

Westmeath

Athlone Castle Visitor Centre

St Peter's Square, Athlone, Co. Westmeath ☎ 090/647 2107,
Ⓦ www.athlone.ie. Daily May–Sept 10am–4.30pm. Adults €5,
children €1.50.

Another castle with a bloody history, the current Norman
edifice sits on top of that erected by Tiordelbach, king of
Connacht, in 1129. The imposing grey walls now hold
nothing more menacing than a visitor centre which docu-
ments the gory action seen during the the Siege of Athlone
in 1690–91 when 12,000 cannonballs destroyed half the
town.

Glendeer Pet Farm

Athlone, Co. Westmeath ☎ 090/643 7147, Ⓦ www.glendeer.com.
Easter & April weekends noon–6pm; May–Sept Mon–Sat
11am–6pm; noon–6pm. Adults €6, children €5.

Just a few miles west of Athlone, residents at this farm
include deer, Vietnamese pot-bellied pigs, ponies, donkeys,
Jersey cows, sheep, goats and peacocks. There are pet animals
to handle, such as puppies, rabbits and guinea pigs, and an
unspoilt nature walk passes historic horse-drawn farm
machinery. As well as a coffee shop, you'll find a play area
with swings, slides, seesaws and a glider swing and indoor
and outdoor picnic areas.

Viking Tours

7 St Mary's Place, Athlone, Co. Westmeath ☎ 090/647 3383,
Ⓦ www.iol.ie/wmeathtc/viking. May–Sept.

A fine and inventive way to get the kids to join you on a
tour out to Lough Ree (afternoon trips from 1pm) or to
Clonmacnoise (a four-hour trip departing 9am); you travel
in a replica longboat and the young ones get to dress up as
Vikings. Prior booking is essential and ticket costs vary
depending upon group size.

Tullynally Castle and Gardens

Castlepollard, Co. Westmeath ☎ 023/46116. Gardens: May–Aug
daily 2–6pm; guided tours of the castle mid–June to July daily
2–6pm. Gardens: adults €5, children €2; gardens & castle:
adults €8, children €4.

Venture through the gatehouse half a mile from
Castlepollard down the road to Granard and you'll find this
beautiful melange of architectural styles based around an
original eighteenth-century tower house. Tullynally Castle
is a masterpiece of landscaped romance set at the end of a

long drive through rolling parkland to the castle itself. The castle is one of the largest in Ireland, largely Gothic Revival in style, with four towers and a long series of battlements. The children should find the vast Victorian kitchen interesting and enjoy the grounds where winding paths lead to lakes, walled gardens and follies, including a Chinese garden. There are tree carvings to look out for and a treasure trail to follow, before you hit the café for tea, coffee and home-made cakes.

Belvedere House, Gardens and Park

Tullamore Rd, Mullingar, Co. Westmeath ☎ 044/49060, ⓦ www.belvedere-house.ie. Daily: May–Aug 9.30am–6pm; March, April & Sept 10.30am–6pm; Oct–Feb 10.30am–4.30pm. Adults €6, children €4, family €17.

Three miles from Mullingar on the N52 road, this elegant hunting and fishing lodge dates from 1740, and its grounds are beautiful; terraces run down to a lake, there are woodlands, a walled garden, an ice house and stables to explore. More modern resources on site include a children's play area, animal sanctuary, tram (open certain days only, adults €1.50, children €1) and coffee shop. The visitor centre features a multimedia presentation about the history of the estate and its restoration.

Longford

Corlea Trackway Visitor Centre

Keenagh, Co. Longford ☎ 043/22386, ⓦ www.heritageireland.ie. April–Sept 10am–6pm. Adults €3.10, children €1.20, family €7.60. Three miles or so from Kenagh village, just off the Kenagh–Longford R397 road. Heritage Card.

Anyone who finds fascination in the ancient past will relish the Corlea trackway, a stretch of oak-built, Iron Age bog road constructed in 148 BC – the largest of its type uncovered in Europe. The visitor centre maintains the excavated 60ft of the path in air-conditioned comfort and places it in context using informative displays on life in the boglands two thousand years ago, a video presentation and informative guided tours that venture outside into the bog of today.

Sports and activities

Adventure centre

Lilliput Adventure Centre Lough Ennell, Mullingar, Co. Westmeath ☎ 044/26789.

Boat cruises

Athlone Cruisers Jolly Mariner Marina, Athlone, Co. Westmeath ☎ 090/6472892, ⓦ www.iol.ie/wmeathtc/acl. Ninety-minute Lough Ree cruises May–Sept. Also rents out cabin cruisers.

Bowling

Mega Bowls Athlone Rd, Longford town, Co. Longford ☎ 043/47643.

Cinema

Mullingar's 6 Screen Cinema Lakepoint Centre, Delvin Rd (N52) Mullingar, Co. Westmeath ☎ 044/85800.

Horse riding

Kells Equestrian Centre Kells, Co. Longford ☎ 046/924 6638. **Moy Riding Centre**, Summerhill ☎ 046/955 7575.

Hot-air ballooning

One-hour trips can be organized from **Glasson Golf Club**, Co. Westmeath or from **Trim Castle**, Co. Meath.
Call the Hot-air Balloon Association: ☎ 01/406 4777 or ☎ 087/933 2622.

Go-karting

Athboy Karting Addinstown, Delvin, Co. Westmeath ☎ 08/806 8776; **Group 8 Karting** Pudden Hill, Ashbourne, Co. Meath ☎ 01/835 4444; **Longford Go Karting** Edgeworthstown, Co. Longford ☎ 043/71308; **Pollard Karting Ltd** Castlepollard, Co. Westmeath ☎ 044/61674.

Swimming

Ceanannas Mor Swimming Pool Navan Rd, Kells, Co. Meath ☎ 046/924 0551; **Longford Swimming Pool** Market Square, Longford town, Co. Longford ☎ 043/46536; **Mullingar Swimming Pool** Mullingar town park (off Austin Friar St), Mullingar town, Co. Westmeath ☎ 044/40262.

Accommodation

The Fincourt Oldcastle, Co. Meath ☏ 049/854 1153, ⓦ www
.fincourt.com. This pub also offers tasteful B&B and self-con-
tained apartment accommodation.

Kells Hostel Kells, Co. Meath ☏ 046/924 9995. Hostel with 4-
bed, 6-bed and 8-bed family rooms – and its own pub.

Kiltale Holiday Homes Kiltale, Dunsany, Co. Meath ☏ 046 943
6679, ⓦ www.meathselfcatering.com. Self-catering accommodation on a working farm. Feed the ducks and hens, bottle-feed
baby goats, pet lambs, collect eggs and cuddle baby chicks and
ducklings. During July and the first two weeks of August a farm
summer camp takes place (Mon–Fri 10am–1pm), when children
are supervised at all times by a qualified teacher and at least
three other adults.

Longford Arms Hotel Main St, Longford town, Co. Longford
☏ 043/46296, ⓦ www.longfordarms.ie. Comfortable accommodation, leisure centre with pool and gym, restaurant and coffee
shop.

Newgrange Hotel Bridge St, Navan, Co. Meath ☏ 046/907
4100, ⓦ www.newgrangehotel.ie. An upmarket option, with a
good restaurant and babysitting available.

Places to eat

Aubergine Gallery Café 1 Ballymahon St, Longford town, Co.
Longford ☏ 043/48633. Contemporary dishes such as
aubergine, feta and olive bruschetta can be half-portions and
there are kid-friendly options such as chicken or sausage and
chips.

Boyle's Tea Rooms Main St, Slane, Co. Meath ☏ 041/982 4195.
Fully licensed and with a range of inexpensive but delicious
home-made food.

Gallery 29 Café, Oliver Plunkett St, Mullingar, Co. Westmeath
☏ 044/49449. Good, inventive café specializing in seasonal spe-
cialities in the organic/free-range line.

The Loft Main St, Kilbeggan, Co. Westmeath ☏ 0506/32243.
Simple, good-value dishes such as baked potato, quiche and
salads in an inviting café.

Woodville House Gaybrook, Mullingar, Co. Westmeath
☏ 044/43694. Country cooking with half-portions half-price;
chicken and chips €8.

5

Louth, Monaghan and Cavan

The border counties of Louth, Monaghan and Cavan are three of the least visited by families holidaying in Ireland, but each certainly has attractions well worth seeing.

Louth is the Republic's smallest county and much of its everyday activity is focused upon the towns of Drogheda and Dundalk. Apart from the small resort of Clogherhead, its coastline is largely undeveloped, though Carlingford, on the

Information

For details of local events and attractions in County Louth visit Ⓦ www.eastcoastmidlands.ie or Ⓦ www.louthholidays .com. Information about the Drogheda area is also available at Ⓦ www.drogheda-tourism.com and for the Cooley Peninsula at Ⓦ www.carlingford.ie. There are tourist offices at Carlingford (Ⓣ 042/937 3033); Drogheda, two offices – Ⓣ 041/983 7070 & Ⓣ 041/984 5684; and Dundalk (Ⓣ 042/933 5484).

Details of events in Co. Cavan can be found at Ⓦ www .cavantourism.com and the county's sole tourist office is in Cavan town (Ⓣ 049/433 1942). Visit Ⓦ www.monaghantourism .com for similar information about Co. Monaghan, whose only tourist office is in Monaghan town (Ⓣ 047/81122).

Cooley Peninsula, is rapidly becoming a very popular holiday spot, thanks to its position overlooking Carlingford Lough and its surrounding good walking countryside. The county also has several important monastic and prehistoric sites.

County Monaghan consists mainly of gently rolling countryside, a mix of rounded hills known as drumlins and tiny lakes, with facilities dotted around or in the towns of Monaghan itself, Castleblayney, Carrickmacross and Clones. Cavan is known for its multitude of lakes and the opportunities offered for boating and angling, as well as fine walking in the west of the county. Its only sizeable centre of population is Cavan town itself, though Ballyconnell, Ballyjamesduff and Belturbet are all pleasant enough in their own right.

All three counties are ideal cycling country. Indeed both Cavan and Monaghan are part of the 230-mile Kingfisher Trail, while the Táin Trail meanders through Louth (☎042/933 5484 for details).

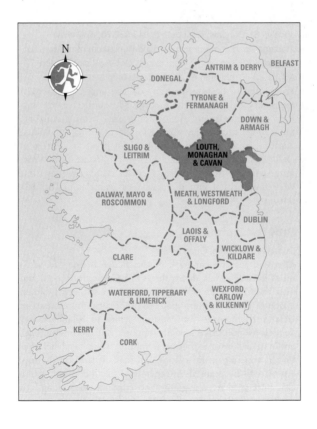

Louth

Millmount Museum

Millmount, Drogheda, Co. Louth ⓣ 041/983 3097, ⓦ www
.millmount.net. Mon–Sat 9.30am–5.30pm, Sun 2–5.30pm.
Museum and tower adults €5.50, children €3, family €12.

The museum sits at the top of Millmount hill, south of the
River Boyne, and provides a superb view of the town of
Drogheda set out below. The Martello tower here dates from
Napoleonic times, but was seriously damaged in 1922 during the Irish Civil War. The collection comprises material on
the town's history, especially its industries, and includes such
exhibits as a Boyne coracle – a circular boat made from a
framework of hazel twigs and the hide of a prize bull – and
a nineteenth-century period kitchen complete with fittings
and fixtures.

Louth County Museum

Jocelyn St, Dundalk, Co. Louth ⓣ 042/932 7056, ⓦ www
.heritageisland.com/attractions/dundalkmuseum.html. Mon–Sat
10.30am–5.30pm, Sun 2–6pm except Oct–April closed Mon.
Adults €3.80, children €1.25, family €10.

In addition to hosting summer concerts and staging regular
temporary exhibitions, the County Museum traces the history of Dundalk and surrounding area from prehistoric
times to the present day, using a variety of formats, including
computerized interactive displays. Of greatest interest to
children will be the Heinkel bubble car, dating from 1966;
using cockpits from German Heinkel bomber planes these
were transformed into three-wheeled vehicles in Dundalk
during the 1960s.

Proleek Dolmen

Dundalk, Co. Louth. Open access.

Accessed via the car park of the *Ballymascanlon Hotel* (3
miles from Dundalk down the R173 Carlingford road) and
near the fifth green of its golf course, the Proleek Dolmen
is one of the most photographed prehistoric monuments in
Ireland. Its huge 46-ton capstone seems to balance rather
dangerously on three upright supports, but the monument's
endurance is proof of its real solidity. One local belief is
that, if you can throw a stone and make it land on the top,
a wish will be granted. Another says that the gallery grave
also here is that of a giant who came from Scotland to
challenge the legendary Finn McCool and came to a sticky
end.

Stephenstown Pond, Agnes Burns Cottage and Visitor Centre

Knockbridge, Dundalk, Co. Louth ☏ 042/937 9019,
ⓦ www.stephenstownpond.com. Stephenstown Pond Nature
Park: daily May–Sept 8.30am–8.30pm, Oct–April 10am–5pm;
free. Cottage and Visitor Centre: daily May–Sept 9.30am–5pm,
Oct–April 10am–3pm; €2.

The result of a community-led initiative, this five-acre site
encompasses pleasant woodland, waterside walks and a pond
stocked with carp (fishing permits available from the visitor
centre). A cottage in the grounds was the home of Agnes
Burns, sister of the Scottish poet Robert Burns. It has been
restored in period style and contains information on both
Robert and Agnes Burns and the latter's working life. The
visitor centre includes an interactive display on Louth's
wildlife and a coffee shop as well as a multimedia room providing Internet access.

Knockabbey Castle and Gardens

Knockabbey, Louth village, Co. Louth ☏ 01/677 8816,
ⓦ www.knockabbeycastle.com. May–Sept Tues–Sun
10.30am–5.30pm. House: adults €6, children €4, family €16;
gardens: adults €6, children €4, family €16; combined: adults
€10, children €8, family €28.

Children are more likely to enjoy the attractive gardens and
the treasure trail (which can be downloaded in advance from
the castle's website) than Knockabbey itself, although there's
a small interpretive centre which explains much of the
house's history as well as the development and restoration of
its gardens. A stroll through their mixture of Victorian
flower gardens and medieval water gardens, alongside buildings such as a pergola and a gazebo, is delightful in sunny
weather.

Monasterboice Round Tower and High Crosses

Monasterboice, Co. Louth. Open access.

If you're travelling northwards along the N1 from Drogheda,
look out for the signs to Monasterboice, about six miles
along the way. In the midst of an old graveyard, situated in a
tranquil, sylvan location, stands one of the tallest round towers in Ireland, rising to a height of 110ft. Its door was originally some 15 to 20ft above the ground and reached by
wooden steps, but the entrance has sunk to ground level
over the ten centuries or so since the tower was constructed.
Unfortunately, you cannot enter the tower for safety reasons.
The other major attraction here is a pair of splendid high
crosses, carved with all manner of decorations depicting

parts of the Bible. Part of the fun in visiting is to try and decipher their meaning; fortunately, there's an information panel available to guide you.

Monaghan

Irish Country Quads

Carrickakelly, Inniskeen, Co. Monaghan ☏ 042/ 937 8997.
Opening times by arrangement. Adults €35 per hour, children €28 per hour.
Older children will thoroughly relish the chance to drive a four-wheeled ATV (All Terrain Vehicle) around the Monaghan countryside. Courses are designed to cater for individual ability and experience and include such thrills as an underground tunnel, various water splashes, tight corners, rugged ground and muddy ditches. Waterproof clothing, boots, gloves and helmets are all provided.

Cavan

Killykeen Forest Park

Killykeen, Co. Cavan ☏ 049/433 2541. Dawn–dusk. Free.
Some 5 miles west of Cavan town off the Killeshandra road, Killykeen Forest Park has plenty of woodland trails and contains historical sites such as the ruined Clogh Oughter Castle. The park is set around the shores of the many intertwining little lakes which actually form the southernmost reach of Upper Lough Erne. There's also a children's play area, tennis courts, boat and bike hire, an equestrian centre and log cabin accommodation (for both see below).

Sports and activities

Activity and adventure centres

Co. Louth: Carlingford Adventure Centre Tholsel St, Carlingford ☏ 042/937 3100, ⓦ www.carlingfordadventure.com; **East Coast Adventure Marina** Carlingford ☏ 042/937 3118, ⓦ www.eastcoastadventure.com; **Neptune Adventure Centre** Clogherhead ☏ 041/983 4422.

Co. Monaghan: Muckno Adventure Centre Lough Muckno Park, Castleblayney ☎ 086/313 1612; **Tanagh Outdoor Education Centre** Dartrey Forest, Rockcorry ☎ 049/555 2988.

Bicycle rental

Irish Cycle Hire Unit 6, Enterprise Centre, Ardee, Co. Louth ☎ 041/685 3772; **Newgrange Bike Hire** 300m from the Brú Na Boinne Centre, Donore, Co. Meath ☎ 086/069 5771; **McQuaid Cycle Hire** Glaslough, Co. Monaghan ☎ 047/88108; **Quay Cycles** 11a North Quay, Drogheda, Co. Louth ☎ 041/983 4526; **Snipe Cycle Hire** Clones, Co. Monaghan ☎ 047/52125.

Cinemas

Diamond Screen Cinema The Diamond, Monaghan town, Co. Monaghan ☎ 047/84755; **Drogheda Omniplex** The Boyne Shopping Centre, Drogheda, Co. Louth ☎ 041/984 4007; **Dundalk IMC** Carroll Village Centre, Dundalk, Co. Louth. ☎ 042/932 0400; **IMC Cinema** Cassore village, Longwalk, Dundalk, Co. Louth ☎ 042/34843; **Omniplex** Abbey Shopping Centre and Boyne Shopping Centre, Drogheda, Co. Louth ☎ 041/984 4007, ⓦ www.filminfo.net; **Storm Cinemas** Main St Car Park, Cavan town, Co. Cavan ☎ 049/437 2005.

Go-karting

Speedway Kart Racing Dublin Rd, Cavan town, Co. Cavan ☎ 049/437 3549.

Horse riding

Co. Cavan: Ashfield Riding Stables Ashfield, Cootehill ☎ 049/555 2045; **Cavan Equestrian Centre** Shalom Stables, Latt ☎ 4049/32017; **Killykeen Equestrian Centre** Killykeen Forest Park ☎ 049/61707; **Lough Sheelin Equestrian Centre** Ross House Mountnugent, Co. Cavan ☎ 049/854 2018; **Redhills Equestrian Centre** Killymare, Redhills ☎ 047/952 6121.

Co. Louth: Beltichburn Equestrian Centre Termonfeckin Rd, Drogheda ☎ 041/983 8063; **Ravensdale Lodge Equestrian and Trekking Centre** Ravensdale, Dundalk ☎ 042/937 1034, ⓦ www.ravensdalelodge.com.

Co. Monaghan: Carrickmacross School of Equitation Drumconrath Rd, Carrickmacross ☎ 042/966 1017; **Castle Leslie Equestrian Centre** Castle Leslie, Glaslough, Co. Monaghan ☎ 047/88256, ⓔ info@castleleslie.com.

Pitch and putt

Co. Cavan: Ballyhaise Pitch and Putt Ballyhaised, ☎ 049/38430.

Co. Louth: Boyne Valley Hotel Stameen, Dublin Rd, Drogheda
℡ 041/984 3280; **Cement Pitch and Putt** Cement Rd,
Drogheda ℡ 041/983 03050; **Channonrock Pitch and Putt
Club** near Louth village ℡ 042/937 4117; **Collon Pitch and Putt
Club** Collon ℡ 041/982 6139; **McBride Pitch and Putt Club**
Weirhope, Drogheda ℡ 086/838 5713; **Seapoint Pitch and Putt
Club** Termonfeckin ℡ 041/988 1315.

Co. Monaghan: Inniskeen Pitch and Putt Inniskeen ℡ 042/937
8230; **Lakeview Pitch and Putt Club** Ardee Rd, Carrickmacross
℡ 042/966 4269; **Malone's Pitch and Putt Club** Muldrummond,
Castleblayney ℡ 042/974 0613; **Monaghan Valley Pitch and
Putt** Killygowan, Monaghan town ℡ 047/84928; **Rowan Springs
Pitch and Putt** Doohamlet, Castleblayney ℡ 042/974 1278.

Swimming

Aura Leisure Centre St Alphonsus Rd, Dundalk, Co. Louth
℡ 042/933 6230; **Bailieborough Swimming and Leisure
Centre** Chapel Rd, Bailieborough, Co. Cavan ℡ 042/966 6644.

Bowling

Astra Bowl Storm Cinema Complex, Townspark, Cavan town,
Co. Cavan ℡ 049/437 2662, Ⓦ www.astra-bowl.com; **Blayney
Bowls** Monaghan Rd, Castleblayney, Co. Monaghan, ℡ 042/974
9944, Ⓦ www.blayney-bowl.com; **Dundalk Sportsbowl**
Racecourse Rd, Dundalk, Co. Louth ℡ 042/933 6000.

Water-skiing

Lough Muckno Water-ski Club Lough Muckno Park,
Castleblayney, Co. Monaghan ℡ 087/666 0077, Ⓦ www
.skimuckno.com.

Accommodation

Boyne Valley Hotel and Country Club Stameen, Dublin Rd,
Drogheda, Co. Louth ℡ 041/983 7737, Ⓦ www.boyne-valley-hotel
.ie. Set in expansive landscaped gardens, southeast of Drogheda
on the N1, the hotel has its own swimming pool and pitch and
putt course. Special midweek deals available.

The Hillgrove Hotel Monaghan town, Co. Monaghan
℡ 047/81288. Modern and comfortable four-star.

Killykeen Forest Chalets, Killykeen Forest Park, Co. Cavan
℡ 049/433 2541, Ⓦ www.coillte.ie/tourism_and_recreation
/killykeen_forest_hols.htm. Self-catering, Scandinavian-style
chalets or log cabins in a tranquil spot.

The Lennard Arms The Diamond, Clones, Co. Monaghan ℡ 047/51075. Very friendly hotel, offering large rooms (some with two double beds) with reductions for children; the downstairs bar also serves splendid meals and has an above-average children's menu.

Riverside Farmhouse Off Cavan Rd, Cootehill, Co. Cavan ℡ 049/555 2150. Very pleasant Victorian house with riverside views with a family room, a triple and three doubles; twenty percent reduction for children.

Shalom Ghan Rd, Carlingford, Co. Louth ℡ 042/937 3151, ⓦ www.jackiewoods.com. Well-equipped B&B by the side of the lake, offering a fifty percent reduction for children.

Places to eat

Andy's Bar and Restaurant 12 Market St, Monaghan town ℡ 047/82277. Hearty lunches and a more exotic evening menu.

Bayleaf Café Main St, Ballyconnell, Co. Cavan. Extremely good-value café and takeaway; open in the evenings too.

The Oystercatcher Bistro Market Square, Carlingford, Co. Louth ℡ 042/937 3922. Serves a variety of seafood and meat dishes.

La Pizzeria Peter St, Drogheda, Co. Louth ℡ 041/983 4208. Exceptionally popular pizza parlour.

The Side Door Restaurant Drumalee Cross, Cootehill Rd, Cavan town ℡ 049/433 1819. Buzzy place serving up pizzas, burgers and steaks.

6

Wexford, Carlow and Kilkenny

T his part of Ireland may not possess huge expanses of bogland, rock and water, but it does have plenty of outstandingly beautiful countryside to entertain family visitors. It also has the advantage of being Ireland's sunniest and driest corner. The landscape is perhaps at its most attractive amongst the valleys and hills of the rivers Nore and Barrow, just north of New Ross and south of Kilkenny city, and is ideal for walking and cycling. Walkers will also love the mountains, valleys and open farmland of the South Leinster Way and the Wexford Coastal Path.

Public transport isn't exceptional, although you can travel to a surprisingly large number of the attractions in the area (the exception being Carlow) by train: the line slices through County Wexford to Wexford city and Rosslare, then continues to New Ross and Kilkenny city via Waterford.

Wexford

Ballyhack Castle and Dunbrody Abbey

Ballyhack, Co. Wexford ⓣ051/389468,
ⓦwww.heritageireland.ie. June–Sept Mon–Fri 10am–1pm,
2–6pm, Sat & Sun 10am–6pm. Adults €1.30, €0.50 children, €4 family. Heritage Card.

Set in picturesque surroundings, this stoutly proportioned five-storey, sixteenth-century tower house makes an ideal starting-point for a family exploration of the area. The castle tower can be climbed to about halfway up its full height, helping build an appetite for the offerings of the rather upmarket seafood restaurant, *The Neptune*, while just to the northeast off the R733 is the ruin of Dunbrody Abbey (daily: April–June & Sept 10am–6pm, July & Aug 10am–7pm; €1.90), which dates from the thirteenth century and makes for a pleasant, post-lunch stroll. There's a handy car ferry from Ballyhack village that'll run Waterford-based visitors back to the village of Passage East across the harbour. Trips take just ten minutes (ⓣ051/382480; €7 single, €10 return).

Enniscorthy Castle and Wexford County Museum

Castle Hill, Enniscorthy, Co. Wexford ⓣ054/35926. Daily:
June–Sept 10am–6pm; Oct–Nov & Feb–May 2–5.30pm, Dec & Jan Sun 2–5pm. Adults €4.50, children €1, family €11.

At the top of Castle Hill overlooking the River Slaney, this formidable, well-preserved and restored Norman castle con-

Tourist offices, open all year unless otherwise stated, are at Wexford city ℡ 053/23111; Enniscorthy ℡ 054/34699 (April–Oct); New Ross ℡ 051/421857 (April–Oct), Rosslare Kilrane ℡ 053/33232 (May–Sept); Carlow town ℡ 059/910503/31554; and Kilkenny city ℡ 056/7751500. Further information on the whole region is available from ⓦ www.southeastireland.ie, on Kilkenny from ⓦ www.kilkenny.ie and ⓦ www. kilkenny.com, on Wexford from ⓦ www.wexfordtourism.ie and on Carlow from ⓦ www.carlow.com.

tains the Wexford County Museum, which has separate rooms displaying different aspects of the region, such as its seafaring, agricultural, industrial, military and ecclesiastical past. There's everything from a mammoth's tooth to blacksmith's tools and 150-year-old sewing machines, and plenty of pikes, bayonets, swords and muskets in the 1798 Room to keep the most military-mad youngster happy. You can also explore an old Irish farm kitchen and a display about early forms of travel as well as seeing old gramophones, a coin collection and even a set of African artefacts. The castle itself has had a colourful history: it served as a prison after the 1798 Rebellion, and a picture of a soldier scratched on a dungeon wall by an imprisoned rebel can still be seen.

National 1798 Visitor Centre

Millpark Rd, Enniscorthy, Co. Wexford ℡ 054/37596, ⓦ www.1798centre.com. March–Sept Mon–Fri 9.30am–6pm, Sat & Sun 11am–6pm; Oct–Feb Mon–Fri 9.30am–4pm. Adults €6, children €4, family €16.

The dramas of the 1798 Rebellion are brought vividly to life at this excellent visitor centre, opened in 1998 to mark the bicentenary of this key event in Irish history, where disorganized rebels around the country, against a background of French Revolution and independence in America, were suppressed at a cost of over 30,000 lives. Audiovisual and interactive exhibits help explain the complicated issues that led up to the insurrection.

Hook Lighthouse, Hook Head Peninsula

Fethard-on-Sea, Co. Wexford ℡ 051/397055, ⓦ www .thehook-wexford.com. March–Oct daily 9.30am–5.30pm; Nov–Feb daily 10am–5pm. Adults €5.50, children €3, family €15.

The bracing Hook Head Peninsula has plenty of isolated spots for picnics, including good sandy beaches, such as Booley Strand, 2 miles to the south of Duncannon. Junior naturalists will enjoy watching the thousands of migrating birds that rest here and may be lucky enough to spot the seals which can sometimes be seen. The beaches are mostly unsuitable for swimming – currents here make it dangerous enough for boats. The tip of the peninsula is the site of Europe's oldest lighthouse – the first having been built here in the twelfth century.

Guillemot Maritime Museum

Kilmore Quay, Co. Wexford ⊤051/561144. Daily: May–Sept noon–6pm; April & Oct Sat & Sun noon–6pm. Adult €4, child €2, family €10.

Exhibits evoke the tough life at sea and are housed in an old 120ft-long, 30ft-wide lightship built in 1922. It's embedded alongside the marina at this small, attractive fishing and holiday village of thatched cottages, whitewashed walls, ice-cream parlours, cafés, restaurants, craft shops and a sandy beach. Children can explore the three levels of the boat, seeing the sailor's cabins, the captain's all-mahogany quarters and the engine room. There are ships in bottles, models of boats made by local sailors going back to 1880 and samples of coral.

Dunbrody Emigrant Ship

South Quay, New Ross, Co. Wexford ⊤051/425239, ⓦwww.dunbrody.com. Daily: April–Sept 9am–6pm; Oct–March 10am–5pm. Adults €6.50, children €4, family €18.

Junior seafarers can test the waters on this magnificent authentic replica of an 1845 three-masted, 458-ton, 176ft-long famine ship, which would have crossed the Atlantic crammed with those escaping Ireland's Great Famine. Audiovisual and interactive displays help to bring the subject of emigration to life, and children get to meet the captain, crew and some of the emigrants telling their stories.

Duncannon Fort Visitor Centre

New Ross, Co. Wexford ⊤051/389454. June–Sept 10am–5.30pm. Adults €4, children €2, family €10.

This huge, star-shaped fortress built in 1584 in anticipation of invasion by the Spanish Armada is a hit with kids, who can climb the ramparts for great views of the harbour. In the summer there are occasional re-enactments of battles and a maritime museum explains the origins of the fishing village of Duncannon. It contains pieces of shipwrecks and several model boats.

Irish National Heritage Park

15 Ferrycarrig, Co. Wexford ⊤053/20733, ⓦwww.inhp.com. Daily March–Oct 9.30am–6.30pm, closing times may vary. Adults €7.50, children 5–16 €3.50, students €6, family €19.

Close to the mouth of the Slaney at Ferrycarrig, this park presents nine thousand years of Irish history using full-scale models of settlements, homesteads, a medieval tower and burial places. Children especially will adore the Mesolithic campsite and Viking shipyard, both brought to life by costumed interpreters.

Irish Agricultural Museum

Johnstown Castle, Bridgetown Rd, Wexford city ℡ 053/42888, ⓦ www.heritageireland.com. April & May Mon–Fri 9am–12.30pm & 1.30–5pm; June–Aug Mon–Fri 9am–5pm, Sat & Sun 11am–5pm; Sept–Nov Mon–Fri 9am–12.30pm & 2–5pm; Dec–March Mon–Fri 9am–12.30pm & 1.30–5pm. Adults €6, children €6, family €20.

The trades of Ireland's past are brought graphically to life by the replica workshops of a blacksmith, wheelwright, cooper, basket-maker and harness-maker. Other child-friendly displays, set in old farm buildings, bring rural ways back to life, and include a travellers' caravan, carriages and machinery. The museum is set in the gardens of Johnstown Castle, a neo-Gothic mansion, and children can explore the grounds (May-Oct) which contain ornamental lakes, hothouses, a statue walk, dark woodlands and walled gardens.

Wexford Wildfowl Reserve

North Slobs, Co. Wexford ℡ 053/23129, ⓦ www.heritageireland.ie. Daily: April–Sept 9am–6pm; Oct–March 10am–5pm. Free.

This wildlife reserve, located at the splendidly named "North Slobs" mud flats, is a magnet for twitchers of all ages. Between October and April they come to see the huge number of migrating birds, notably white-fronted geese from Greenland. The visitor centre provides excellent preparation for viewing wildfowl on the reserve, which is well furnished with hides and lookout towers. The reserve is signposted off the Gorey road (R741) north out of Wexford.

Dunmore Cave

Castlecomber Rd, Ballyfoyle, Co. Kilkenny ℡ 056/776 7726. March to mid-June & mid-Sept to Oct daily 9.30am–5.30pm; mid-June to mid-Sept 9.30am–6.30pm; Nov–Feb Sat & Sun 9.30am–5.30pm. Admission by guided tour only. Adults €2.75, children €1.25, family €7.

This cave is 7 miles north of Kilkenny (the N77 road and then the N78) on an isolated limestone outcrop of the Castlecomer plateau; kids love the experience of climbing the many steps down into the stalagmite- and stalactite-ridden cave, which resembles a 1950s science fiction film. In 928 AD it was thought to be the site of a Viking massacre. Although Ireland has larger caves to visit, Dunmore is well lit and easily accessed. The sleek and modern visitor centre by the cave has several displays and there is an excellent introductory film that, despite explaining in depth how the cave was formed, manages to captivate even the youngest viewers.

Kilkenny

Kilkenny Castle grounds

The Parade, Kilkenny city ☎ 056/772 1450, ⓦ www .heritageireland.ie. Daily: April–May 10.30–5pm; June–Aug 9.30–7pm; Sept–March 10.30am–12.45pm & 2–5pm. Adults €5 children €2, family €11.

While the tours of the castle itself largely focus on fine art, children are likely to be more interested in the gardens and parkland, which include a playground and riverside walk.

Nore Valley Park Open Farm

Bennettsbridge, Co. Kilkenny ☎ 056/772 7229, ⓦ http://norevalleypark.tripod.com/farm. April–Sept Mon–Sat 9am–8pm. Adults €4.50, children €4.30, family €4 per person.

This is a great day out for the family – as well as plenty of animals there's a straw-covered playing area, a playground with swings and slides as well as pedal go-karts, crazy golf and trailer rides. Children are encouraged to feed the animals and can view them from an American-style fort in the grounds.

Sports and activities

Adventure park

Pirates Cove Adventure Park Courtown Harbour, Co. Wexford ☎ 055/25555. An adventure golf course with a pirate theme, plus computerized ten-pin bowling and large-scale radio-controlled models of trucks, safari cars and pirate ships.

Bicycle rental

Co. Wexford: Arthurstown Youth Hostel Arthurstown ☎ 051/389411; **The Bike Shop** 9 Selskar St, Wexford ☎ 053/22514; **Kenny's Bike** Slaney St, Enniscorthy

054/33255; **Kilmore Quay Bike** Island View House, Kilmore Quay ☎ 053/29781.

Co. Carlow: Celtic Cycling, Bagenalstown ☎ 0503/75282; **A.E. Coleman** 19 Dublin St, Carlow ☎ 0503/31273.

Co. Kilkenny: **J.J. Wall** Maudlin Street, Kilkenny ☎ 056/772 1236.

Boat rental and cruises

Dick Hayes Kilmore Quay, Co. Wexford ☎ 053/29704, 0872 549111. Mr Hayes and his boat can be hired for €350 per six-hour day for up to ten people; individuals (adults and children both cost €50), based on availability, and from June–Sept hiring the boat for €150 for three-hour evening trips is popular with families.

Galley Cruising Restaurant New Ross, Co. Wexford ☎ 051/421723, ⓦ www.rivercruises.ie. Boat trips run from Easter to October up the Barrow and Nore.

Valley Boats Graiguenamanagh, Co. Kilkenny ☎ 0503/972 4945. Barges and narrow boats for hire by the week, for €700–1400 depending upon size and time of year.

Wexford Harbour Trips Trips around Wexford harbour cost €7 per person and run throughout the summer. Book through *Kirwan House Hostel*, 3 Mary St, Wexford ☎ 053/21208.

Horse riding

Boro Hill Equestrian Centre Clonroche, Co. Wexford ☎ 054/44117; **Horetown House Foulksmills** Co. Wexford ☎ 051/565771; **Seaview Trekking Centre** Hook Head, Co. Wexford ☎ 051/562239; **Shelmalier Riding Stables** Wexford (☎ 053/39251).

Leisure centres

Forest Park Leisure Centre Courtown, Gorey, Co. Wexford ☎ 055/24849. Three swimming pools and water slide.

Quad biking

Country Quads Tinnecarrig, Borris, Co. Carlow ☎ 059/972 4624; **Quad Attack** Clonroche, Enniscorthy, Co. Wexford ☎ 054/44660.

Accommodation

Hibernian Hotel 1 Ormonde St, Kilkenny; ☎ 056/777 1888, ⓦ www.kilkennyhibernianhotel.com. Upmarket hotel with leisure centre and pool for rainy days.

Kelly's Resort Hotel Rosslare, Co. Wexford ☎ 053/32114, ⓦ www.kellys.ie. A hotel that especially welcomes families with excellent sporting facilities including a pool, indoor tennis and squash as well as miniature golf and a playground.

St Margaret's Beach Caravan and Camping Park Rosslare, Co. Wexford ☎ 053/31169. Close to the beach and particularly welcoming to families.

Talbot Hotel Trinity St, Wexford ☎ 053/22566, ⓦ www .talbothotel.ie. Pleasant, family-oriented, three-star hotel with leisure centre, swimming pool and babysitting facilities.

Places to eat

Antique Tavern Enniscorthy, Co. Wexford ☎ 054/33428. On the quayside, this popular pub decorated with Wexford memorabilia, including mounted elk heads and a glass case containing money from around the world, offers simple meals like sandwiches and soups.

Cappuccino's 23 North Main St, Wexford ☎ 053/22311. Good-value Mediterranean snacks, burgers and baguettes.

M.L. Dore 65 High St, Kilkenny. Well-established café with inexpensive snacks, sandwiches, cakes, etc.

Into The Blue 80 South Main St, Wexford ☎ 053/22011. Inexpensive snack bar and restaurant with generous sand-wiches and bagettes (€4), fajitas and paninis (€6) and children's portions available on dishes such as pasta or curry (€9.50).

Italian Connection Parliament St, Kilkenny ☎ 056/7764225. Good Italian food such as kiddies' favourites pizza and pasta in a convivial, if a little dark, atmosphere.

Key Largo Canal St, Kilkenny ☎ 056/23922. Inexpensive, with vegetarian dishes, pasta, pizza, salads, fajitas.

Lennon's Café Bar 121 Tullow St, Carlow ☎ 059/913575. Prize-winning and stylish gastropub.

7

Waterford, Tipperary and Limerick

These three counties are ideal for a restful rural stay rather than for visiting a wide range of sites. Co. Waterford boasts a southern border of more than fifty miles of coastland which is characterized by extensive bays, secluded beaches and cliffs, while inland the farm and hilly woodland is broken up by the Comeragh, Monavullagh and Knockmealdown mountains. This is excellent walking and cycling country, along with the Ballyhoura and Galty mountain ranges of Tipperary, and the Mullaghareirk peaks of Limerick.

The area is well served by railways: the diagonal line from Limerick to Waterford via Clonmel couples with another from Cork to Portlaoise via Thurles to form a huge cross

Information

Co. Waterford: Dungarvan ☎ 058/41741; Lismore ☎ 058/54975; Waterford city ☎ 051/875823.

Co. Tipperary: Cahir ☎ 052/41453 (April–Sept); Carrick-on-Suir ☎ 051/640200; Cashel ☎ 062/61333 (May–Sept); Clonmel ☎ 052/26500; Nenagh ☎ 067/31610 (mid-May to mid-Sept); Tipperary Town ☎ 062/33466 (May–Sept).

Co. Limerick: Adare ☎ 061/396255 (Feb–Dec); Limerick city ☎ 061/317522.

through the region, its diagonals meeting near Tipperary town. There are airports at Waterford and Shannon, just northwest of Limerick city, while trunk roads connect all the main centres. Buses connect Dublin with most main towns and with each other.

Waterford

Waterford Crystal Glass Factory

Kilbarry, Co. Waterford ☎ 051/332500, ⓦ www
.waterfordvisitorcentre.com. Tours daily: March–Oct 8.30am–
6pm; Nov–Feb Mon–Fri 9am–5pm. Booking advised. Adults €6,
under 12s free, but no under 10s permitted in the factory.
Children and adults alike are mesmerized by displays of
skilled glass-blowing alongside the hot furnaces. Guided
tours of this world-famous factory last an hour and include
glass-cutting, engraving and sculpting and there is a film on
the history of glass making in Ireland.

Reginald's Tower

The Quay, Waterford city ☎ 051/304220. Daily: Easter–May &
Oct–Nov 10am–5pm; June–Sept 9.30am–6pm; Dec–Easter
Wed–Sun 10am–5pm; adults €2, children €1.

Originally built by the Vikings, Reginald's Tower has existed
on Waterford Quay for more than a thousand years, during
which it has functioned as a fortress, a mint and a prison. It
now holds a new exhibition about its own past and that of
the Viking and medieval periods. Today's tower dates back to
the twelfth century, and has been completely restored to its
medieval magnificence.

Waterford Treasures

Merchant's Quay, Waterford city ☎ 051/304500, ⓦ www
.waterfordtreasures.com. Daily: April–Sept Mon–Sat
9.30am–6pm, Sun 11am–6pm; Oct–March Mon–Sat 10am–5pm,
Sun 11am–5pm. Adults €4, children 5-16 €2, family €10.

A splendid museum detailing the city's history from Viking
times onwards through seven audiovisual presentations
(including a 3-D audiovisual sea voyage) and interactive displays and plenty of interesting artefacts, including Viking and
Anglo-Norman jewellery and weaponry mostly dug up in
the last twenty years.

Tipperary

Mitchelstown Cave

Burncourt, Cahir, Co. Tipperary ☎ 052/67246,
ⓦ www.mitchelstonecaves.com. Daily: Feb–Oct 10am–6pm;
Nov–Jan 11am–5pm. Adults €4.50, children €2, family
€12.50.

The guided tour of these impressively damp and echoing
caves takes you half a mile through three large caverns with
stalactites, stalagmites, calcite crystals and a 30ft-high calcite
column.

Cahir Castle

Cahir, Co. Tipperary ☎ 052/41011, ⓦ www.heritageireland.ie.
Daily: mid-March to mid-June & mid-Sept to mid-Oct
9.30am–5.30pm; mid-June to mid-Sept 9am–7pm; mid-Oct to
mid-March 9.30am–4.30pm. Adults €2.75, children €1.25, family €7. Heritage Card.

A magnificent, well-preserved castle situated on a rocky
island on the River Suir that variously dates from the thirteenth to the nineteenth century. It has all the extras chil-

dren expect, such as a keep complete with portcullis and vaulted chambers, a moat, dark spooky walks, a prison accessed by a trap door, plenty of turrets and musket loops. There's a short video on the locality and a coffee shop.

Ormond Castle

Carrick-on-Suir, Co. Tipperary ☎051/640787. Daily mid-June to mid-Sept 10am–6pm for guided tours. Adults €2.75, children €1.25, family €7. Heritage Card.

A beautiful Elizabethan mansion tacked onto the remains of a fourteenth-century castle complete with two towers built in the mid-fifteenth century.

Brú Ború, Cultural Centre

Cashel, Co. Tipperary ☎062/61122, ⓦwww.comhaltas.com. Mid-June to mid-Sept Mon 9am–5pm, Tues–Sat 9am–9pm; mid-Sept to mid-June Mon–Fri 9am–5pm. Exhibition: adults €5, children €3, entry to centre free.

Buried in chambers 20ft below the Rock of Cashel, the Sounds of History exhibition (a bit heavy-going for the under 10s, to be honest) examines Ireland's traditional music from ancient times onwards. There are performances of traditional Irish music (mid-June to mid-Sept, Tues–Sat 9pm), which your younger ones might enjoy.

Cashel Folk Village

Dominick St, Cashel, Co. Tipperary ☎062/62525. Daily: March–April 10am–6pm; May–Oct 9.30am–7.30pm. Adults €3.50, children €1.

Located in the lane behind the tourist office, this museum has items relating to Republican history as well as a gory reconstruction of a butcher's shop, a pub, a forge and so on.

Rock of Cashel

Co. Tipperary ☎062/61437, ⓦwww.heritageireland.ie. Daily: mid-March to mid-June 9am–5.30pm; mid-June to mid-Sept 9am–7pm; mid-Sept to mid-March 9am–4.30pm. Adults €5, children €2, family €11. Heritage Card.

One of the top six visitor attractions in Ireland, a staggering sight from a distance and equally enthralling when you get there, the Rock of Cashel is a huge limestone outcrop upon which rises a collection of medieval Christian buildings including a cathedral, church, round tower and castle tower house. In contrast with these majestic sites, a mile out on the road to Clonmel is the tiny Bothan Scoir (☎062/61360; visits by prior arrangement), a miserable seventeenth-century one-roomed peasant dwelling.

Parson's Green Leisure Park

Clogheen, Co. Tipperary ☎ 052/65290, ⓦ www.clogheen.com.
Mid-March to Sept 10am–8pm. Adults €3, children €2, family
€10.

By the Knockmealdown Mountains, this riverside attraction features farm and pet animals including sheep, goats,
emus and llamas, an agricultural museum, woodland walks,
crazy golf, boat trips, pony rides, playgrounds and a coffee
shop.

Museum of Transport

Richmond Mill, Clonmel, Co. Tipperary ☎ 052/29727. Mon-Sat
10am–6pm, also June–Aug Sun 2–6pm. Adults €3.50, children
€2, family €8.

Displays at this small museum include vehicles going back to
the 1930s, such as Rolls-Royces, Fords and Jaguars, as well as
motorbikes, petrol pumps, road signs and other motoring
memorabilia.

Folk Farm and Transport Museum

Fethard, Co. Tipperary ☎ 052/31516. Sun noon–6pm & by
appointment. €2.50.

At the start of the Cashel road, this museum housed in a former railway station has twelve hundred exhibits including
hearses, horse-drawn carriages, penny farthings and other
bicycles, Victorian prams and everyday household items from
a century ago.

Nenagh Heritage Centre

Nenagh, Co. Tipperary ☎ 067 33850. April–Oct Mon–Fri
9.30am–5pm. Free.

Once North Tipperary's county gaol, and later a school,
today this building houses models of Lough Derg and two
lakeside villages – Dromineer and Garrykennedy. Fascinating
though these miniature worlds are, expect the family to
come away ruminating on the condemned cells, the gloom
of the prison, and the pithy biographies of some of those
whose lives ended here.

Limerick

King John's Castle

Nicholas St, Limerick city ☎ 061/360788, ⓦ www
.shannonheritage.com. March, April & Oct 9am–5pm; May–Sept

9am–5.30pm; Nov–Feb 10.30am–4.30pm. Adults €7.95, children €4.20, family €17.50.

One of Ireland's best Anglo-Norman castles, despite the modern entrance spoiling the huge gateway. Kids will love dragging their parents up to the battlements for panoramic views of the city. There are displays of medieval weaponry, a twenty-minute film on the history of the city and an interpretive centre focusing on the Normans in Ireland.

Celtic Theme Park and Gardens

Cloonagulleen, Kilcornan, Co. Limerick ☎ 061/ 394243. Daily mid-March to Oct 9.30am–6pm. Adults €6, children under 12 free.

Situated on an original Celtic settlement, Celtic Park helps to interpret Ireland's ancient past. On display are a stone circle, mass rock, dolmen, lake dwelling, cooking site, stone templar church, lime kiln, holy well, ogham stone, communal tomb and Celtic chieftain's chair. The coffee shop enjoys panoramic views of the surrounding West Limerick countryside.

Stonehall Visitor Farm

Curraghchase, Pallaskenry, Co. Limerick ☎ 061/ 393940, Ⓦ www.stonehallvisitorfarm.com. April, May, June & Sept Sat & Sun noon–6pm; July & Aug Mon–Sat 11am–6pm, Sun noon–6pm. €5.

Located in a tranquil and beautiful rural setting, with a wide variety of animals. On rainy days kids can enjoy the indoor play area with tractor and trailers, rough riders and monkey magic bouncing castle.

Foynes Flying-Boat Museum

Foynes, Co. Limerick ☎ 069/65416, Ⓦ www.flyingboatmuseum.com. Daily: April–Oct 10am–6pm; Nov 11am–4pm. Adults €5, children €2.50.

This museum celebrates late 1930s and early 1940s Foynes when the town was a staging post for the transatlantic flying-boat service. Children will enjoy the radio and weather room, where original transmitters, receivers and Morse Code equipment are on show.

Croom Mills

Croom, Co. Limerick ☎ 061/397130, Ⓦ www.croommills.ie. Daily: May–Sept 10am–6pm; Oct–April 10am–5pm. Free.

The large cast-iron water-wheel of this corn-grinding mill is powered by the River Maigue. There is a century-old steam engine, alongside interactive exhibits and a video about the history of Croom Mills and the milling process – plus a restaurant.

Lough Gur Visitor Centre

Near Bruff, Co. Limerick ℡061/360788, Ⓦwww
.shannonheritage.com. Daily May–Sept 10am–6pm. Adults
€4.75, children 0–5 free, 6–18 €2.95, family €13.50.

Tells the story of the pre-Celtic settlers of Ireland who
farmed in this peaceful valley, their dwellings, rituals and
burial sites. The visitor centre houses an exhibition of artefacts and display panels as well as an interpretive audiovisual
show.

Sports and activities

Bicycle rental and tours

Emerald Cycles 1 Patrick St, Limerick ℡061/416983.
Murphy Cycles Main St, Dungarvan ℡058/41376, Ⓦwww
.irelandrentabike.com.
Easy Wheelin Cycle Tours, ℡051 390706 or ℡086 3745809,
Ⓔeasywheelingtours@yahoo.co.uk. Guided cycle tours around
Co Waterford, South Wexford and South Kilkenny.

Boat cruises

Galley River Cruises Waterford ℡051/421723. Lunch (€20;
2hr), dinner (€38; 3hr) and evening tea (€10; 2hr) river trips to
New Ross from June to August; children have a third off.

Horse riding and pony trekking

Hillcrest Equestrian Centre Hillcrest House, Gallbally, Co.
Limerick ℡062/37915; **Homeleigh Farmhouse**, Ballinacourty,
Glen of Aherlow, Co. Tipperary ℡062/56228; **Tipperary
Mountain Trekking Centre** Rusheen, Borrisoleigh, Nenagh, Co.
Tipperary ℡0504/51055.

Recreation centre

Leisure Zone Family Recreation Centre Williamstown, Waterford
city, Co. Waterford ℡051/872 466, Ⓦwww.leisurezone.ie. Ten-pin
bowling, American pool, and skating at the Winter Garden – the
only year-round skating rink in the Republic of Ireland.

Swimming

Civic Swimming Pool Borstal Square, Clonmel, Co. Tipperary
℡052/21972; **Splashworld** Tramore, Co. Waterford
℡051/390176, Ⓦwww.splashworld.ie.

Water sports and adventure sports

Dunmore East Adventure Centre Dunmore East Harbour, Co. Waterford ☎ 051/383783, ⓦ www.dunmoreadventure.com. Summer camps for 10- to 17-year-olds and various adventure sports including windsurfing, sailing, canoeing, climbing and archery.

Oceanic Manoeuvers Tramore, Co. Waterford ☎ 051/390944, ⓦ www.oceanicmanoeuvers.com. Adult and children's lessons, summer camps, certificate courses, group surf packages, guided beach walks and treasure hunts.

Seapaddling.com Unit 112, Dunhill Enterprise Park, Dunhill, Co Waterford, ☎ 087/2686529 or ☎ 051/358995, ⓔ info @seapaddling.com, ⓦ www.seapaddling.com. Full- and half-day sea kayaking trips around the Waterford coastline.

Tramore Bay Surf and Wildlife Centre The Beach, Tramore, Co. Waterford ☎ 051/391297, ⓦ www.surftbay.com. Home of Ireland's largest surf club, T-Bay Surf Club was established in 1967. Features a surf school and an environmental and wildlife visitor centre.

Accommodation

Cashel Holiday Hostel 6 John St, Cashel, Co. Tipperary ☎ 062/62330, ⓦ wwww.cashelhostel.com. A good, centrally located hostel.

Clonea Strand Hotel Clonea, Dungarvan, Co. Waterford ☎ 058/45555, ⓦ www.clonea.com. The hotel complex has a holiday cottage for seven plus a leisure centre with swimming pools, tennis, ten-pin bowling and playgrounds.

Homeleigh Farmhouse, Ballinacourty, Co. Tipperary ☎ 062/56228. Four miles south of Tipperary, a B&B that also offers pony trekking and fishing.

Kilmaneen Farmhouse, Clonmel, Co. Tipperary ☎ 052/36231, ⓦ www.kilmaneen.com. Easter–Sept. *Kilmaneen* offers comfortable B&B accommodation, on a remote working dairy farm with good walks, and two-bedroom self-catering cottage.

McEniss Ard Rí Hotel Ferrybank, Waterford City ☎ 051/832111, ⓦ www.jurysdoyle.com. Although this chain hotel is rather bland, there are extensive grounds, a leisure centre with pools, a gym for rainy days, babysitting and a kids' room in July and August. Overlooks both the city and the River Suir.

Park House Farmhouse Stradbally, Co. Waterford ☎ 051/293185. Ideal for secluded sandy Stradbally Cove.

Places to eat

Bella Italia 43 Thomas St, Limerick ☎061/418872. Italian-style bistro serving freshly made pasta and pizza and sauces served in a modern setting.

The Green Onion Old Town Hall, Rutland St, Limerick ☎061/400710.Trendy restaurant offering an extensive menu. Closed Mon & Sun.

Haricot's Wholefood Restaurant 11 O'Connell St, Waterford ☎051/841299. Cosy, good-value café with staples such as pasta, vegetable soup and lentil casserole from €8.50, half-portions €5.

Mr Bumbles Kickham St, Clonmel, Co. Tipperary ☎052/29188. Informal eatery with anything from coffee and cakes to full steak suppers.

Moll Darby's 8 George's Quay, Limerick ☎061/411511. Superb international and traditional Irish cuisine in a quay-side setting

The Parrish 41–42 Mary St, Dungarvan, Co. Waterford ☎058/45700. Inexpensive but good snacks and meals including sandwiches, soups, potato wedges and panini, €3–5.

Racket Hall Country House Hotel Dublin Rd, Roscrea ☎0505/21748. An old-world country residence situated in the heart of Ireland's midlands, just outside the Heritage Town of Roscrea. An à la carte pub menu is served until 10pm daily.

The Tannery 10 Quay St, Dungarvan, Co. Waterford ☎058/45420. Modern menu that, though not cheap, is very good value for money. Children welcome until 8.30pm.

Texas Steakout 116 O'Connell St, Limerick ☎061/410350. Wild West theme restaurant with an international and vegetarian menu and full bar licence.

8

Cork

ork is Ireland's largest county and one of the most popular with families visiting the country. As well as the lively and charming port city of Cork, there's beautiful mountain scenery, peaceful lakes, and a

coastline of spectacular cliffs, quiet beaches and coves to enjoy.

Although the railway will only really take you off to visit other counties to the north, the roads are at their best in the south of County Cork, and buses reach everywhere important.

Blarney Castle

Blarney, Co. Cork ⓣ 021/438 5252, ⓦ www.blarneycastle.ie.
May & Sept Mon–Sat 9am–6.30pm, Sun 9.30am–5.30pm;
June–Aug Mon–Sat 9am–7pm, Sun 9.30am–5.30pm; Oct–April
Mon–Sat 9am–6pm/sunset, Sun 9.30am–sunset. Adults €7.

Just a few miles northwest of Cork, this castle, built in 1446, is notable for housing the famous Blarney Stone, which even quite young visitors will queue up for, so that they can be dangled over. Legend suggests that a kiss of the stone will give you the gift of the gab, and its fame has caused the town to grow into something of a tourist centre. You may have to wait an hour for your chance at the stone during the summer months. Be warned, it's sited some 80ft above the ground; you'll need a head for heights to reach it.

Cork city centre

Cork city is built on an island, and is ideal for wandering around to take in the sights and atmosphere. The centre is sandwiched between two channels of the River Lee and there are plenty of cafés, restaurants and interesting shops to look at, as well as Crawford Municipal Art Gallery (Emmet Place, Mon–Sat 10am–5pm; free) with its impressive collection of Irish art. The English Market off Princes Street is worth a detour on your wandering, for the food stalls and the delicious products on sale.

Cork Gaol

Convent Ave, Sunday's Well, Cork city, Co Cork ⓣ 021/430
5022, ⓦ www.corkcitygaol.com. Daily: March–Oct 9.30am–6pm;
Nov–Feb 10am–5pm. Adults €5, children €3, family €14.

Suitable for all ages, the atmosphere of this former prison is re-created using life-size wax figures and eerie sound effects. The exhibition looks in depth both at heroes of the early republican era – who stayed here before being transported to Australia – and at stories of the ordinary men, women and children locked up from the pre-Famine era to the foundation of the Irish state, often for crimes that would now seem quite trivial, in conditions of unimaginable cruelty.

Cork Heritage Park

Blackrock, Cork city, Co Cork ⓣ 021/435 8854. May–Aug

around noon–5pm Thurs–Sun, opening times can vary. Adults €5, children €3, family €10.

As well as the many animals to be seen in the pet farm, aviary and duck pond, there is an activity centre where children can draw and paint, with exhibitions on the Cork Fire Service and the city's maritime history.

St Anne's Shandon

Shandon St, Cork city, Co. Cork ☎ 021/450 5906. Mon–Sat May–Sept 10am–6pm; Oct–April 10am–5pm. €5.

This prominent church sits nearby the old butter market at the top of a hill overlooking the River Lee. Children will love it not only for its weather vane, an eleven-foot gold fish, but for its tower, which can be climbed for a great view and a ring of the bells.

Dursey Island cable car

Mon–Sat 9–11am, 2.30–5pm & 7–8pm and variable Sun.

On a windy day kids and parents will be filled with excitement as they take the six-minute cable-car ride across the slim sound from the furthest tip of the Beara Peninsula to Dursey Island. The views make it an unforgettable experience. Even though there's nothing to do on the island but enjoy the bracing walks and look at the houses, it makes for a memorable day. The cable car has room for just three passengers and a cow, so you may have to go in two groups, and you'll find it at the end of the R572 road.

Queenstown Story

Cobh Heritage Centre, Railway Station, Cobh ☎ 021/481 3591, ⊛ www.cobhheritage.com. Daily: May–Oct 10am–6pm; Nov–April 10am–5pm. Adults €5, children €2.50, family €15.50.

Few children's ears don't prick up at the mention of the *Titanic* which stopped at Cobh on its tragic maiden voyage, one of the subjects covered at this multimedia attraction. *The Lusitania*, her sister ship, also stopped off here on her final voyage, which also ended in tragedy; she was torpedoed and sank with equally massive loss of life (many victims were buried at Cobh). This action led directly to the US joining World War I. The port was also a departure point for those destined for the Napoleonic Wars, for emigrants heading to America and for convicts transported to Australia in the nineteenth century. Further insight into Cobh's dramatic past can be found at the Cobh Museum (Easter–Oct Mon–Sat 11am–1pm & 2–6pm, Sun 3–6pm; €1.50).

Fota Wildlife Park and Fota House

Fota Island, Carrigtwohill, Co. Cork ☎ 021/481 2678, ⓦ www.fotawildlife.ie. Summer Mon–Sat 10am–5pm, Sun 11am–5pm; winter Mon–Sat 10.30am–3.30pm, Sun 11am–3.30pm. Adults €10.50, children €5.50.

This park, 10 miles from Cork city (off the N25 road or Fota's own station on the Cork city-Cobh line), has more than ninety species in open surroundings, with those not in cages left free to roam. There are playgrounds, a tour train, gift shop and self-service café, as well as the Fota Arboretum and Gardens adjacent. Fota House (ⓦ www.fotahouse.com; April–Sept Mon–Sat 10am–5.30pm, Sun 11am–5.30pm, Oct–March 11am–4pm; adults €5, children €2, family €12), which sits in the middle of the grounds, is of limited interest to most children. It's a smart, early nineteenth-century hunting lodge. Rooms on show include the dining room, the hall and its gallery, and the servants' quarters.

Charles Fort

Summer Cove, Kinsale, Co. Cork ☎ 021/477 2263, ⓦ www.heritageireland.ie. Mid-March to Oct 10am–6pm; Nov to mid-March Sat & Sun 10am–5pm. Adults €3.50, children €1.25, family €8.25.

Built between 1678 and 1682, this star-shaped fortress was involved in one of Ireland's most important historical events, the Williamite War (1689–92). The main attraction as far as the kids are concerned are the interactive exhibits, which let them have a go at designing a fort of their own, using the touch-screen displays.

Schull Planetarium,

Schull ☎ 028/28315 or 28552, ⓦ http://homepage.eircom.net/~planetarium. Christmas holidays, Easter weekend, bank holidays and May–Sept: phone for details. Adults €4.50, children €3.20, family ticket (two adults and two children) €12. Shows last for 45min and are unsuitable for children under 7.

Perched next to the harbour, this is the only planetarium in the country, built by the enthusiastic amateur stargazer, Josef

Menke. The late Herr Menke enjoyed many holidays in Cork with his family and built the planetarium in this tiny fishing village as a permanent "thank you". It opened in 1989 and, since then, "The Starshow" has been a great success, and a must-see attraction. All shows are presented by experienced lecturers, who welcome questions from children and adults in the sessions immediately afterwards.

Skibbereen Heritage Centre

Upper Bridge St, Skibbereen, Co. Cork ⓣ 028/40900, ⓦ www.skibbheritage.com. Mid-April to mid-May & mid-Sept–Oct Tues–Sat 10am–6pm; mid-May to mid-Sept daily 10am–6pm. Adults €4.50, children €2.50.
Located in the beautifully restored old gasworks building, the heritage centre contains exhibitions, dramatizations and interactive exhibits on the Great Famine, which greatly affected the town (there are mass graves at Abbeystrewery nearby, where almost 10,000 are buried). An interpretive centre explains the unique marine life of nearby Lough Hyne, a landlocked salt lake, with a saltwater aquarium containing species from the lake.

Fox's Lane Folk Museum

Fox's Lane, Youghal, Co. Cork ⓣ 024/91145. July–Sept Tues–Sat 10am–1pm & 2–6pm; open by appointment rest of year. Adults €4, children €2, family €10.
This museum, tucked away in the centre of a holiday resort town, is home to more than six hundred domestic appliances and gadgets. Dating from around 1850 to 1950, the exhibits include gramophones, old-style telephones, cast-iron sewing machines, immensely heavy typewriters, vacuum cleaners, and more unusual items such as cucumber straighteners, a wasp trap and petrol-fuelled clothes irons. Children find all this ancient quirky history fascinating and a visit here should entertain the parents too.

Perks Family Entertainment Centre

Seafield Business Centre, Youghal, Co. Cork ⓣ 024/92438, ⓦ www.perksfunfair.com. Free admission, prices for activities vary.
Kids can really let their hair down here. There are funfair rides (including a ghost train and crazy mirrors), snooker, pool, ten-pin bowling, video games, an ice-cream parlour and fast-food restaurant to entertain them for hours.

Sports and activities

Bicycle rental

An Stór Hostel Drury's Avenue, Midleton ☎021/463 3106;
CycleScene 396 Blarney St, Cork ☎021/430 1183; **MTM
Cycles** 33 Ashe St, Clonakilty ☎023/33584; **Rothar Cycles** 55
Barrack St, Cork ☎021/431 3133; **N.W. Roycroft and Son** Ilen
St, Skibbereen ☎02821235.

Boat rental and cruises

Atlantic Boating Service Baltimore ☎028/22734,
ⓦwww.atlanticboat.ie. You can rent a motor-boat here that will
seat six or so for €250 per week or €65 per day.

Harbour Queen Ferries Glengarriff ☎027/63116. Ten-minute
trips past basking seals to Garinish Island cost €10 for adults,
and €5 children. If you want to visit the island, too, there's an
additional charge (adults €3.50, children €1.25).

Marine Transport Services Atlantic Quay, Cobh ☎021/481
1485. Harbour boat trips, June–Sept, adults €5, children €3.

Naomh Ciarán Ferries Baltimore ☎028/39135. Ferry trips to
Clear Island, taking 45min, adults €11.50 return, children €6.

Horse riding

Bantry Horse Riding Bantry ☎027/51412. Classes and treks
for children as well as adults.

Swimming

Gus Healy Swimming Pool Douglas Rd, Cork ☎021/429 3073;
Leisureworld, Rossa Avenue, Bishopstown, Cork ☎021/434
6505.

Water sports and adventure sports

Atlantic Sea Kayaking Union Hall ☎028/33002, ⓦwww
.atlanticseakayaking.com. River and sea kayaking trips and
courses.

Sea Kayaking Garrettstown, Kinsale ☎021/477 8884.

International Sailing Centre Cobh ☎021/481 1237,
ⓦwww.sailcork.com. Sailing, powerboating (over 12s only) and
canoeing courses.

Oysterhaven Activity Centre Kinsale ☎021/477 0738,
ⓦwww.oysterhaven.com. Sailing, windsurfing, canoeing,
kayaking and equipment/boat rentals.

Trabolgan Holiday Village Midleton ☎021/466 1551. All-
weather entertainment including archery, abseiling, badminton,
basketball, crazy golf and swimming. Closed Nov–March.

West Cork Sailing Centre Adrigole ☎ 027/60132. Kayaking, powerboating, sailing.

Accommodation

An Stór Hostel Drury's Ave, Midleton ☎ 021/463 3106. Dorms, twins and family rooms in a converted mill.

Barley Cove Holiday Park Crookhaven ☎ 028/35302; Easter & May to mid-Sept. Accommodation is in self-catering mobile homes. Convenient for a great beach, the park also has tennis courts, a café/takeaway and bicycles for rent.

Bay View House Old Timoleague Rd, Clonakilty ☎ 023/33539, ⓦ www.bayviewclonakilty.com; closed Nov–Feb. Immaculate, bright B&B with a 33 percent reduction for kids.

Jurys Cork Inn Anderson Quay, Cork ☎ 021/427 6444, ⓦ www.jurysdoyle.com. Accommodation of a high standard that is especially good value for families. Rooms can accommodate two adults and two children under 12.

Westlodge Hotel Bantry ☎ 027/50360, ⓦ www.westlodgehotel.ie. Upmarket modern hotel with pool, gym, tennis and squash, self-catering cottages and organized family activities June–Aug.

Places to eat

Kalbo's Bistro 48 North St, Skibbereen ☎ 028/21515. Informal, offering good-value lunches such as baguettes and baked potatoes from about €8.

Pak Fook Youghal ☎ 024/90668. Chinese food, always a winner with children.

Pizza Republic 97 South Main St, Cork ☎ 021/427 9969. Laid-back, moderately priced bistro with a wide choice including kids' pizza and pasta dishes for €6.

Quay Co-op 24 Sullivan's Quay, Cork ☎ 021/431 7026. Vegetarian/vegan self-service café for breakfast, lunch, tea, dinner and children's portions.

Spanish Point Restaurant Ballycotton ☎ 021/464 6177. Well-appointed overlooking Ballycotton Bay; children can get half-portions of the €23 lunches, such as chicken and chips and pasta dishes.

9

Kerry

I t is not difficult to fathom why Kerry is eternally popular with visitors: it contains some of Ireland's best scenery, made up of rugged coastline, mountain, moorland and lakes, coupled with a great choice of accommodation and places to eat. True, sections of the county get overrun by

Tourist offices are at Dingle ☎066/915 1188; Kenmare ☎064/
41233 (April–Oct); Killarney ☎064/31633; Listowel ☎068/
22590 (June–Sept); and Tralee ☎066/712 1288.

tourism at times, especially around the 110-mile Ring of
Kerry, Ireland's most popular scenic route. Yet the crowds and
tourist kitsch are always easy to escape, and it's an ideal place
to enjoy a great variety of family entertainment, from swimming and beachcombing to cycling, boating and water sports.

Roads and therefore bus routes fan out in all directions
from the two main towns, Tralee and Killarney, and a railway
line stretches from Tralee to Killarney and the east.

Crag Cave

Castleisland ☎066/714 2144, ⒲www.cragcave.com. Daily: mid-
March–June & Sept–Oct 10am–6pm; July & Aug 10am–6.30pm.
Adults €6.50, children €4, family €20.

This well-lit network of limestone caves, discovered in 1983,
is more than a million years old. It extends two miles underground and the thirty-minute guided tour passes numerous
stalactites and stalagmites. There is an indoor play area for
children aged under 9 (extra charge) as well as craft shop and
café.

Coolwood Park

Coolwood, Coolcaslagh, Killarney, Co. Kerry ☎064/36288.
June–Sept 11am–6pm, weather permitting. Adults €4, children
€3, family €17.

This wildlife park and sanctuary has all kinds of birds and
beasts, some of which children can take part in feeding.
There are also nature walks, a coffee shop and a playground
with slides, swings and climbing frames.

Oceanworld

Mara Beo, Dingle ☎066/915 2111, ⒲www.dingle-oceanworld.ie.
Daily 10am–6pm. Adults €8.50, children €5.50, family €23.

This centre for marine conservation on the waterfront is not
massive, but still has around thirty tanks including a touch
pool, a tropical coral reef display in the shark tank and a tunnel tank to walk through. There is a new turtle exhibition
and children can help feed the fish. Staff walk around the
aquarium with some creatures, such as lobsters and crabs, so
that they can be seen up close. After seeing more than a
hundred species of fish and other marine life, holding a
starfish and stroking a ray, you can take a walk along the
beautiful Dingle Peninsula.

CASTLEISLAND • COOLWOOD • DINGLE

Kennedy's All-weather Pet Farm and Playground

Glenflesk, Killarney, Co. Kerry ☏ 064/54054. April–Oct
10am–7pm; Nov–March 10am–5pm. €6 per person.

Five miles from Killarney town centre on the N22 Cork
road, this working dairy and sheep farm also has puppies,
kittens, rabbits, pigs, goats, ducks, geese, donkeys, and many
more birds and animals. Many can be handled and fed by
visitors. There are free pony rides, indoor and outdoor playgrounds and traditional farm machinery on display.

Killarney National Park

Killarney, Co. Kerry. Visitor Centre: mid-March to June, Sept &
Oct daily, 9am–6pm; July & Aug daily 9am–7pm. Free.

About a third of this beautiful park is made up three lakes
and almost parallel to its western border is a glacial breach
called the Gap of Dunloe. There is a visitor centre at
Knockreer House with a twenty-minute audiovisual about
the park, along with other information. Bicycles can be
hired in Killarney, and there are various tours by a combination of boat, pony trap, bus and bike, and guided walks on
foot. Enquire at Killarney tourist office.

Muckross Estate

Muckross, Killarney, Co. Kerry ☏ 064/31440, ⓦ www
.muckross-house.ie. House: daily 9.30am–5.30pm. Farms: mid-
March to April & Oct, Sat & Sun 1–6pm; May daily 1–6pm;
June–Sept daily 10am–7pm. Joint ticket for house and farms:
adults €8.25, children €3.75, family €21; friary: mid-June to
early Sept daily 10am–5pm; free; gardens: open all year; free.

The various attractions of Muckross Estate combined can
make for a pleasing, if not ecstatic, day for the family. Muckross
House is a nineteenth-century neo-Elizabethan mansion,
livened up somewhat for visitors by its installation of crafts-
people demonstrating such things as weaving, bookbinding
and pottery. There is also the ruin of a Norman and Gothic
friary, extensive gardens, walks to Muckross Lake, a good café-
restaurant in the crafts centre and three traditional working
farms where actors reconstruct day-to-day farming life in
years gone by and such activities as potato picking, harvesting
and hay-making can be seen, depending on the time of year.
Children can also experience a trip on a vintage coach.

Museum of Irish Transport

East Avenue Rd, Killarney, Co. Kerry ☏ 064/34677. Daily:
March–Oct 10am–6pm; Nov–Feb 11am–4pm. Adults €5, children €2, family €12.

This excellent museum has plenty of well-preserved vintage
cars including the world's rarest car, the Silver Stream, built

in 1907, of which only one was manufactured. There are also fire engines, carriages, bicycles and motorbikes, as well as a 1930s workshop.

Fenit Sea World

The Pier, Fenit, Tralee, Co. Kerry ☎066/713 6544. Daily Easter–Oct 11am–5.30pm. Adults €5.50, children €3.50, family €17.50.

Aquarium with marine life from Tralee Bay and the Atlantic Ocean. Kids might be more interested in the timbers of a haunted shipwreck, a submarine labyrinth and a re-creation of the gloomy ocean floor.

Kerry the Kingdom at Kerry County Museum

Ashe Memorial Hall, Denny St, Tralee, Co. Kerry ☎066/712 7777, ⓦwww.kerrymuseum.ie. Jan–March Tues–Fri 10am–4.30pm; April–May Tues–Sat 9.30am–5.30pm; June–Aug daily 9.30am–5.30pm; Sept–Dec 9.30am–5pm. Adults €8, children €5, family €22.

Accounts of the history of Ireland and Kerry from the first settlers in 8000 BC to the declaration of the Irish Republic in 1948. Audiovisual presentations, reconstructions and archaeological treasures as well as temporary exhibitions are livened up by the Irish Medieval experience, a re-creation of streets and buildings of fifteenth-century Tralee.

Scanlon's Pet Farm

Ballydavid, Tralee, Co. Kerry ☎066/915 5135. Mid-April to Sept Mon–Fri 10am–6pm, Sun 2–6pm. Adults €3, children €1.50, family €10.

Surrounded by countryside and overlooked by Mount Brandon, this farm has animals that include deer, geese, pigs, peacocks and rabbits, many of which can be fed by children in the mornings. There are indoor and outdoor playgrounds, river walks and a picnic area.

Tralee to Blennerville Steam Railway and Blennerville Windmill

☎066/712 1064 or ☎066/712 8899. Train: April–Sept, Tues–Sun hourly, but check first; return adults €5, children €2.50.
Windmill: April–Oct daily 10am–6pm; adults €4, children €2.

You can still travel this section of the Tralee-Dingle line, which ran from 1891 to 1953, a fifteen-minute journey, at the end of which is Blennerville Windmill, Ireland's biggest working windmill. There's the usual exhibition on the locality, with audiovisuals and craft workshops, but it's the windmill itself that's the real attraction.

Sports and activities

Bicycle rental

Altazamuth Valentia Island ☎ 066/947 6300; **Casey's** Main St, Cahersiveen, ☎ 066/947 2474; **Glenross Caravan and Camping Park** Glenbeigh ☎ 066/976 8451, ⓦ www.killarneycamping.com (mid-April to Oct); **O'Sullivan's Cycles and Outdoor Store** Bishop's Lane, New St, Killarney ☎ 064/31282; **Tralee Gas Supplies** Strand St, Tralee ☎ 066/712 2018.

Boat trips and ferries

Blasket Ferries Ventry ☎ 066/915 6422. Boats to Great Blasket Easter–Oct, €20 return.

Flannery's Dingle ☎ 066/915 1967. Offers two-hour boat trips (€15, wetsuit hire €20) enabling participants to swim with Fungi, Dingle harbour's resident dolphin.

Seafari Kenmare ☎ 064/83171; ⓦ www.seafariireland.com. Five cruises from the pier July–Aug, with the possibility of spotting whales, seals and dolphins. Children get to enjoy a puppet show, sweets and face painting too.

Skellig Heritage Centre Portmagee ☎ 066/947 6306, ⓦ www.skelligexperience.com. Cruises around Skellig Michael Island (1hr 45min; €21) and Knightstown and around the harbour (1hr; €17), the price includes the exhibition on the locality at the heritage centre.

Valentia Island Ferry Reenard Point ☎ 066/947 6141. Frequent till 10pm April–Sept. Cars return €7, cyclists return €3, pedestrians €2.

Horse riding

Killarney Riding Stables Killorglin Rd, Ballydowney, Killarney ☎ 064/31686, ⓦ www.killarney-reeks-trail.com. Horse riding in the county's national park for adults and children aged over 8. One hour costs €25 per person.

Long's Ventry ☎ 087/225 0286. From €20 per hour for mountain and beach riding, minimum age 8.

Quad biking

Waterville Quad Safari and War Game Adventures ☎ 066/947 4465, ⓦ www.actionadventurecentre.com. There's a combat game for those aged 10 and over (€55).

Swimming

Aqua Dome Tralee ☎ 066/712 8899, ⓦ www.discoverkerry.com/aquadome. Adults €10, children €9.

Huge water slides, wave and whirl pools, rapids and water cannons, and next door 18-hole miniature golf course, Aqua Golf.

Water sports and adventure sports

Cappanalea Outdoor Education Centre Killorglin ☏ 066/976 9244. Canoeing, windsurfing, rock-climbing and other outdoor activities.

Jamie Knox Watersports Castlegregory ☏ 066/713 9411, ⓦ www.jamieknox.com. Activities like surfbiking, paddle-boating and snorkelling. Canoeing, for example, €6 per hour; five-session windsurfing course for under 12s, €120.

Accommodation

Gleneagle Hotel Kenmare Rd, Killarney ☏ 064/36000, ⓦ www.gleneagle-hotel.com. The good leisure facilities, pool and restaurants make this a nice family choice.

Glenross Caravan and Camping Park Glenbeig ☏ 066/976 8451, ⓦ www.killarneycamping.com. May to mid-Sept. Lots of facilities including shop, laundries, TV and games rooms, plus forest and riverside walks.

Killarney International Hostel Aghadoe Rd, Killarney ☏ 064/31240. Three miles northwest of the centre and ideal for the mountains; there are family rooms, bike rental and a free bus to and from the bus and train stations.

Places to eat

The Bricin 26 High St, Killarney ☏ 064/34902. Cosy restaurant with traditional Irish food on the menu like boxties (potato pancakes). Adult meals €14–20 and set two courses €21 with half-portions for kids. Also children's menu, €6.

The Moorings Portmagee ☏ 066/947 7108, ⓦ www.moorings.ie. Restaurant and bar, averaging €35 for three-course meal with children's menu (chicken nuggets and chips, etc) €5.

Out of the Blue Strand St, Dingle ☏ 066/915 0811. Seafood deli and restaurant with outside tables and child-sized portions.

QC's 3 Main St, Cahersiveen ☏ 066/947 2244; winter Thurs–Sun only. Very accommodating place which features a children's menu with chicken nuggets/fishfingers and chips €6.50. Adult meals €12.

10

Clare

W ith some of Ireland's most stunning landscapes,
County Clare provides visitors with a wide range of
experiences, from the musical traditions kept very
much alive in energetic Ennis, the lively county
town, to the bleak tranquillity of the Burren, a seemingly

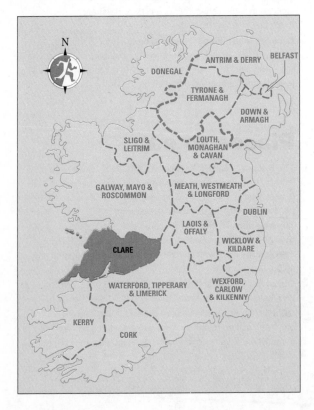

Tourist offices are at Ennis ☏ 065/682 836); Killaloe ☏ 061/
376866 (May–Sept); and Kilkee ☏ 065/905 6112 (mid-May to
early Sept). The official website, at ⓦ www.shannonregiontourism
.ie, has all the latest information.

endless expanse of limestone and shale. The coast is scattered
with wonderful sandy beaches and little seaside villages and
there are plenty of opportunities for water sports. The county has plenty of gentle farmland, which is ideal for cycling.
The many small lakes north of Dysert O'Dea are ideal for
fishing.

A spider's web of roads spread out from Ennis, in the centre of the county, and there are up to eight daily trains from
Ennis to Limerick (1hr) and to Dublin (3hr). Buses serve
most areas daily, and run at least hourly during the day to
and from Bunratty, Ennis and Limerick to Shannon Airport.

Aillwee Cave

Ballyvaughan, Co. Clare ☏ 065/707 7036, ⓦ www.aillweecave.ie.
Daily 10am–6pm. Adults €10, children €5, family €30.
The surprise underground world of this fascinating limestone cave formed in a prehistoric ice age in the Burren is
revealed in the thirty-minute tours over bridged chasms,
caverns of stalagmites and stalactites, a frozen waterfall, curi-
ous rock formations and hibernation chambers of extinct
brown bears. A thundering waterfall occasionally sprays visitors and children will enjoy looking out for the calcite formations in the form of such things as praying hands and a
wasp's nest. Back outside the cave children can stretch their
legs on a nature trail through woodland. As well as a gift
shop and tearoom, cheese can sometimes be seen being
made in the dairy or honey being extracted from combs.

Newtown Castle

Ballyvaughan, Co. Clare ☏ 065/707 7200. May–Sept
10am–4pm. Free.
This sixteenth-century fortified tower has all the features
that children find interesting – battlements, narrow slit windows, gun loops and "murder holes", while the nature trail
adjacent to the castle takes you on a mile-long trip around
the Burren.

Bunratty Castle and Folk Park

Bunratty, Co. Clare ☏ 061/360788,
ⓦ www.shannonheritage.com. Daily: Jan–March & Nov–Dec

9.30am–5.30pm; April–Oct 9am–5.30pm. Combined ticket for castle and folk park: adults €11, children €6.25, family €28.85.

A strategically important site since Viking times (970 AD), the existing castle is Ireland's most complete medieval castle. Built in 1460 it boasts a well-restored keep. Bloodthirsty fledgling knights can discover the dungeon and inspect the castle's "murder holes", where attackers would be met with a barrage of boiling water or oil. The folk park, although perhaps over-touristy, brings history to life for little ones by re-creating a nineteenth-century village complete with a watermill, church, ten farmhouses, a schoolhouse, doctor's house, merchant buildings and shops. There is a forge, printing press and bakery, as well as costumed characters.

Riches of Clare Exhibition

Clare Museum, Arthur's Row, Ennis, Co. Clare ⓣ065/682 3382, ⓦwww.clarelibrary.ie. June–Sept Mon–Sat 9.30am–5.30pm, Sun 9.30am–1pm; Oct–May Tues–Sat 9.30am–1pm & 2–5pm. Free.

This sleek, permanent exhibition in the county's modern museum makes intelligent use of interactive displays, informative commentary and lively audiovisual presentations to throw light on the past. Packed with intriguing items that range from an ancient human hip bone pierced by a prehistoric arrow to examples of more modern weaponry used by the IRA, and including Clare's connection to the Spanish Armada, the museum also has a traditional hearth scene where children can sit and listen to an old Clare folk tale. A good day's worth of entertainment all in one building.

Knappogue Castle

Near Quin, Ennis, Co. Clare ⓣ 061/360788, ⓦwww.shannonheritage.com. Daily April–Oct 9.30am–5.30pm. Adults €5.95, children €3.

A wonderfully restored fifteenth-century castle that puts on its own medieval banquets (April–Oct 6.30pm). There is also a newly restored nineteenth-century walled garden and formal garden for your little lords and ladies to let off steam.

The Craggaunowen Project

Kilmurry, near Quin, Co. Clare ⓣ061/360788, ⓦwww.shannonheritage.com/Craggaunowen_Day.htm. April to mid-Oct 10am–6pm. Adults €7.50, children €4.50, family €18.50.

Craggaunowen explains how the Celts arrived and lived in Ireland. There are replicas of an Iron Age road, a fourth-century ring fort, a hunter's cooking site and a Crannog, a Bronze Age lake dwelling made from wattles, reeds and mud. Craggaunowen Castle, built in 1550, stands on a crag overlooking the lake, and a replica of the "Brendan Boat", built and sailed from Ireland to Greenland by Tim Severin to echo the voyage of St Brendan, who was reputed to have discovered America long before Columbus.

The Burren Centre

Kilfenora, Co. Clare ⊤065/708 8030, ⊛www.theburrencentre.ie. Mid-March to May, Sept & Oct 10am–5pm; June–Aug 9.30am–6pm.

A combination of models of castles and forts, and touch-screen and audiovisual displays including an effective 3-D map of the Burren region and a film tracing its evolution, and explanations of the natural history, plant and animal life, geology and archaeology of this famously harsh region.

Lahinch Seaworld

Lahinch, Co. Clare ⊤065/708 1900, ⊛www.lahinchseaworld.com. Daily, opening times vary. Swimming, sauna and Jacuzzi: adults €7, children 5–16 €5, children 2–4 €3; aquarium only: adults €7, children 5–16 €5, children 2–4 €3; combined swimming and aquarium tickets: adults €12, children 5–16 €8, children 2–4 €4; playzone: under 12s €4.

Lahinch effortlessly provides a complete family day out with its aquarium featuring a ray pool, wave tank, touch pools, lobster breeding station, ocean tank and more, while kids can play at being fish themselves in the 25-metre swimming pool and kiddies' pool. Finally, there's a playzone for the under 12s featuring crawl tubes, a tube slide, ball pools and pendulum swings.

Moher Hill Open Farm and Leisure Park and Cliffs of Moher

Cliffs of Moher Rd, Liscannor, Co. Clare ⊤065/708 1071, ⊛www.moherfarm.com. May–Sept 10am–6pm, Oct & April weekends and by appointment. €5.

A good day out guaranteed: as well as the many inmates here, including sheep, deer, llamas, goats, donkeys and ponies, there are indoor and outdoor play areas, which feature go-karts, sand diggers, mini golf and a bouncy castle. Close by Liscannor, the Cliffs of Moher stretch for five miles, and are Clare's most majestic natural attraction. Accessible by well-marked footpath, they should not be missed.

West Clare Railway

Moyasta Junction, Kilrush, Co. Clare ⊤065/905 1284; ⊛www.westclarerailway.com. Mon–Sat 10am–6pm, Sun noon–6pm. Adults €6, children €3.

Dolphin watching

There are few better ways for children to appreciate the beauty and charm of these wonderful creatures than by meeting them close up, but from the safety of a boat. Numerous companies offer dolphin-watching excursions, but these are among the best:

Dolphinwatch The Pier, Carrigaholt ⓣ 065/905 8156, ⓦ www.dolphinwatch.ie. Runs daily two-hour trips from mid-March to end Oct, to see the resident group of bottlenose dolphins. Very child-friendly, there's even a toy box on board. Adults €20, children 4–16 €10.

Dolphin Discovery Kilrush, Co. Clare ⓣ 065/905 1327, ⓦ www.discoverdolphins.ie. This firm has a boat purpose-built for watching the Shannon Estuary bottlenose dolphins, equipped with a hydrophone so you can listen to them as well. Tours run May–Sept; adults €17, children €8.

A section of this 112-year-old narrow-gauge railway line operates for tourist trips through the Clare countryside. Passengers get to ride in carriages built in the style of that period, pulled by a diesel locomotive. As well as the four-mile trip, visitors see the refurbished railway station and 1950s film of the train operating.

Sports and activities

Bicycle rental

Gleesons Henry St, Kilrush ⓣ 065/905 1127; **Williams** Circular Rd, Kilkee ⓣ 065/905 6041.

Boat cruises and rental

Derg Princess Killaloe Heritage Centre, The Canal, Killaloe ⓣ 065/376866. Hour-long cruises of Lough Derg May–Sept daily noon & 2.30pm. €7.

Lakeside Watersport Caravan and Camping Park Mountshannon ⓣ 061/927225. Canoe (€10 per hour), sailboat (€22 per day) and motor boat (€40 per day) rental May–Oct.

Whelan's Boat Hire Main St, Killaloe ⓣ 061/376159. Boats for four with outboard engines.

Horse riding and pony trekking

Burren Riding Centre Fanore ⓣ 065/707 6140. Riders aged 8 and over, €20 per hour.

Clare Equestrian Centre Deerpark, Doora, Ennis ⓣ065/ 684 0136, Ⓦ www.clareequestrian.com. Treks starting from €20 per child, classes and pony camps.

Clonara Equestrian Centre Oakfield, Clonara ⓣ061/354172. Indoor and outdoor arenas, lessons, trekking and cross-country.

Swimming

Waterworld Circular Rd, Kilkee ⓣ065/905 6855. Kid-friendly pool with 200ft tower slide. Mon–Fri, noon–7pm; Sat–Sun 2–8pm. Closed end Oct–Easter.

Traditional Irish music

Glór Irish Music Centre Friar's Walk, Ennis ⓣ065/684 3103, Ⓦwww.glor.ie. A national centre for the performance of Irish music with regular performances, some specifically aimed at children. Film, theatre, dance, visual arts and children's workshops also.

Water sports and adventure sports

Killaloe Activity Centre Killaloe ⓣ061/376622. Hires out wind-surfs, wetsuits, dinghies and canoes.

Kilkee Diving and Watersports Centre Kilkee ⓣ065/905 6707. Scuba-diving, prices vary.

Kilrush Creek Lodge and Adventure Centre Cappa Rd, Kilrush ⓣ065/905 2855, Ⓦwww.kcac.nav.to. Kayaking, canoe-ing, windsurfing, powerboating, archery, raft-building, orienteer-ing and sailing. Typically €15 per hour, €50 per day per activity.

Accommodation

Nagle's Camping and Caravan Park Doolin, Co. Clare ⓣ065/707 4458; April–Sept. Tremendous location between the Burren and the Cliffs of Moher.

West County Hotel Clare Rd, Ennis ⓣ065/682 3000, Ⓦwww.lynchotels.com. A modern hotel less than a mile south of the centre with three swimming pools and a children's play centre. Rooms can accommodate two adults and two children.

Places to eat

Bofey Quinn's Main St, Corofin ⓣ065/683 7321. Family-friendly restaurant with wide selection of dishes including children's menu from €6.

Ruby Tuesday's Merchants Square, Ennis ☎ 065/684 0474. Good-value restaurant with family-friendly feasts such as pastas, chicken nuggets/burger and chips, around €10 adults, €3.95 children.

Strand Restaurant Kilkee ☎ 065/905 6177, ⓦ www .clareguesthouse.com. On the seafront with good seafood and meat dishes (€16–25 adult) and a small selection of dishes for kids (€5.50).

Whitethorn Restaurant Whitehorn Visitor Centre, Ballyvaughan ☎ 065/707 7044; mid-March to Oct. Good food in a great setting, with children's portions.

11

Galway, Mayo and Roscommon

alway is a popular holiday destination for many visitors: the lively, culturally rich city of Galway, with its modern beach resort Salthill, is a convenient base for the splendid scenery of west Galway, notably the untouched wilderness of Connemara and its seemingly endless bog, heather-clad moorland and mountain. The region is also home to fourteen Blue Flag beaches, four on Achill island, one on a freshwater lake at Loughrea, and the rest at Bertra, Carrowroe, Clare Island, Elly Bay, Kinvara, Mulranny, Old Head (Louisburgh), Ross (Killala), and Inishmore. Children, particularly, will love the adventure of taking a ferry across to the sandy beaches of the stark Aran Islands, Inishmore, Inishmaan and Inisheer. Roscommon and Mayo, in contrast, are often overlooked as a holiday destination yet offer restful rural delights. Mayo is renowned among anglers, and boasts four great lakes as well as one of Ireland's most popular resort towns, Westport.

Information

Tourist offices are open all year unless otherwise stated, at Galway ☎ 091/537700; Tuam ☎ 093/25486 (mid-June to mid-Sept); Inishmore ☎ 099/61263; Oughterard ☎ 091/552808; Roundstone ☎ 095/35815 (summer); Clifden ☎ 095/21163 (March–Oct); Inishbofin ☎ 095/45861 or 45895; (summer); Westport ☎ 098/25711; Cashel ☎ 098/47353; Killala ☎ 096/32166 (July–Sept); Vallina ☎ 096/70848; Foxford ☎ 094/925 6488; Cong ☎ 092/46542 (March–Oct); and Roscommon ☎ 0903/26342.

The region is well served by public transport. From Athlone a railway line stretches to Galway, with another reaching Westport via Roscommon and Claremorris, and a further line branching from Claremorris to Ballina. Roads and therefore buses reach most extremes of the three counties, with Galway being the greatest travel hub by far.

Galway

National Children's Discovery Museum

Ballybrit Industrial Estate Upper, Galway ☎ 091/766829, ⓦ www.childrensdiscoverymuseum.ie. June–Aug Sat–Wed 10am–5pm, Thurs–Fri 10am–7pm; Sept–May Tues–Sun 10am–5pm. Adults €4, children €7, family €26.
Especially designed for children of 12 years and under. Using a hands-on interactive approach, children learn about themselves and their world. Visit grandmother's living room, dress

up in exciting costumes and perform on stage, or stand inside a giant-sized bubble. Climb into a giant mouth, try crafts, produce your own play or broadcast from the media room.

Dan O'Hara's Homestead and the Connemara Heritage and History Centre

Lettershea, Clifden, Co. Galway ⓣ 095/21246, ⓦ www
.connemaraheritage.com. April–Oct daily 10am–6pm. Adults €6, children €3.

This centre features a restored cottage and homestead, and reconstructions of a ring fort and lakeside dwelling all viewable by guided tour by tractor-bus. There are turf-cutting demonstrations, sheep-herding and other activities demonstrated for groups on request, as well as a twenty-minute video on the history of the region, archaeological displays, a craft shop and tearoom.

Atlantaquaria

Toft Park, Salthill, Galway, Co. Galway ⓣ 091/585100,
ⓦ www.atlantaquaria.com. April–Sept daily 10am–6pm;
Oct–March Wed–Fri 10am–5pm, Sat & Sun 10am–6pm. Adults
€7.50, children €4.50, family €22.

This excellent aquarium includes a miniature version of Galway's waterways complete with docks, locks and salmon piers, and displays of native Irish aquatic life, with both seawater and freshwater fish. A child's perspective is always present, for example in the story of an Atlantic salmon's adventures en route for Greenland and back again.

Connemara National Park

Near Letterfrack, Co. Galway ⓣ 095/41054. Visitor centre: mid-March to May, Sept & Oct 10am–5.30pm; June 10am–6.30pm; July & Aug 9.30am–6.30pm. Adults €2.75, children €1.25.

Situated in the heart of the west of County Galway, this beautiful area covers 2000 hectares of mountains, bog, heath and grassland. The visitor centre on the west side of Letterfrack village introduces the history, geology, wildlife and plantlife of the park and is the starting-point of several nature trails. An eighteen-minute audiovisual presentation traces the natural history of Connemara and during July and August there are organized children's days with art, fun and games with nature as the theme.

Ocean's Alive Sealife Centre

Letterfrack, Co. Galway ⓣ 095/43473. Daily March–Sept
10am–7pm. Aquarium and museum: adults €5, children €2.50;
aquarium, museum and cruise: adults €15, children €10.

Principally a maritime museum, this also has a small aquarium with fish of the locality including starfish and rockpool dwellers. Shipwrecks, boats and maritime artefacts such as lobster pots and model boats explain local maritime history, and you can take an hour-long wildlife cruise to nearby uninhabited islands.

Athenry Castle

Athenry, Co. Galway ⓣ091/844797, ⓦwww.heritageireland.ie.
April, May & mid-Sept to Oct Tues–Sun 10am–5pm; June to mid-Sept daily 10am–6pm. Adults €2.75, children €1.25, family €7.

Athenry's Norman walls give the town a fortified, medieval feel that kids will love, and the thirteenth-century castle boasts a fantastic three-storey keep. A further Athenry distraction is the heritage centre (daily 10am–6pm; ⓣ091/844661, ⓦhomepage.tinet.ie/~athenryheritage/heritagecentre/heritage.htm; €3.50), situated in the eighteenth-century church of St Mary's, with audiovisual displays of the castle's history. Children can dress up in medieval costume, try archery or get lost in the maze.

Dartfield Horse Museum

Dartfield, Killreekill, Loughrea, Co. Galway ⓣ91/843968, ⓦwww.dartfieldhorsemuseum.com. Daily 9am–6pm. €5.

Showing the use of the horse through history, this isolated museum, surrounded by fields and paddocks, contains displays demonstrating the importance of the horse in the areas of transport, farming, sport and local traditions. Children can use the bank of computers to glean further equine information, and there is a rather tame riding machine, small play area, café and shop with riding gear and souvenirs.

Turoe Open Farm and Leisure Park

Bullaun, Loughrea, Co. Galway ⓣ091/841580, ⓦwww.turoefarm.com. Daily Easter–Sept 10am–7pm; Oct–Easter Sat & Sun, public hols & half-terms 1.30–6pm. Adults €5, toddlers €7, children €10.

Animals to cuddle and feed, a nature trail, indoor and outdoor playgrounds, bouncy castles, play maze and more. Balloon modelling and clowning, picnic areas and seasonal entertainment for the whole family.

Glengowla Mine

Oughterard, Co. Galway ⓣ091/552360. March–Nov daily 9.30am–6.30pm. Adults €6.50, children €3.50.

Lively guided tours evoke the tough lives miners endured working by candlelight in this lead and silver mine worked between 1850 and 1865. They were often knee-deep in water, blasting the rock and drilling by hand. You can see many of the workings of the mine, including original ladders, pulley systems and pipes. On the surface is a blacksmith's workshop and cottage.

Mayo

Tumble Jungle

Ballina, Co. Mayo ⓣ096/76637, ⓦwww.tumblejungle.ie.
Holidays Mon–Sun 10am–7pm; school term Wed–Sun
10am–7pm. €6.50 per child per 1.5hr, 1–12 years.
This is Ireland's largest indoor play centre and features a huge space with five bouncy castles, a climbing frame with a two-storey obstacle course, a soft play area for toddlers and a café.

Maghu's Castle

Kiltimagh, Co. Mayo ⓣ094/9374886. July–Aug Mon–Fri
noon–6pm; Sept–May Sat noon–6pm, Sun 2–6pm and at selected other times. €5 per child per hr 1–11 years.
This new all-weather playground has everything the desperate parent could need on a rainy day: an adventure maze, rope bridge, slide, ball pond, aerial runway, punch bags and toddlers' play area.

Westport House

Westport, Co. Mayo ⓣ098/27766, ⓦwww.westporthouse.ie.
March–Oct 11.30am–5pm. Adults €15, children €10, family
€49.
The main attractions for children of this grand stately home built in 1730 are the mini-railway, the giant water slide and bouncy castle in the grounds. If that isn't enough, there are pedaloes, train rides, pitch and putt, rowing boats and an indoor play area. Add the dungeons (complete with spooky sound effects) and bird and animal park, and you've got a full, fun day out for all the family.

National Museum of Ireland – Country Life

Turlough Park House, Turlough, Castlebar, Co. Mayo
ⓣ01/6777444, ⓦwww.museum.ie/countrylife. Tues–Sat
10am–5pm, Sun 2–5pm. Free.
This is the first branch of the National Museum to open outside Dublin. The exhibitions portray the lives of ordinary people who lived in rural Ireland from 1850 to 1950. The

house was designed in the High Victorian Gothic style and is home to the Irish Folklife Collection of over 50,000 objects reflecting Irish traditional life, largely of a rural nature. The collection includes objects dealing with agriculture, fishing and hunting, clothing, architecture, vernacular furniture, trades and crafts, transport, sports and leisure and religion. The museum runs regular activities and workshops for ages 7+ on topics as diverse as making St Brigid's crosses, basket-weaving, blacksmithing, decorating Easter Eggs, treasure hunts and Hallowe'en festivities. There is no cost for these, but pre-booking is essential.

Roscommon

King House

Main St, Boyle, Co. Roscommon ⓣ 071/966 3242, ⓦ www.roscommoncoco.ie/kinghouse. Daily April–Sept 10am–6pm. Adults €5, children €3, family €15.

Lifesize models and special effects trace the history of this elegant Georgian house. Children are encouraged to participate, whether dressing as a Gaelic chieftain or building a brick vault. Afterwards they can tackle the on-site adventure playground.

Glendeer Pet Farm

Drum, Athlone, Co. Roscommon ⓣ 090/643 7147, ⓦ www .glendeer.com. Easter to end Sept Mon–Sat 11am–6pm, Sun noon–6pm; Dec Ireland's Lapland Mon–Fri 5–8pm, Sat &Sun 3–8pm. €6.

Glendeer's six-acre open farm boasts over fifty species of animals and birds, a play area and picnic area. The farm is transformed into Ireland's Lapland for the month of December with Santa, live deer, Dancer and Prancer, a crib and a snow scene.

Sports and activities

Bicycle rental

John Mannion Bridge St, Clifden, Co. Galway ⓣ 095/21160;
Sean Sammo, James St, Westport, Co. Mayo ⓣ 098/25471;
Mill House American St, Belmullet, Co. Mayo ⓣ 097/81181;
Cong Hostel Headford Rd, Cong, Co. Mayo ⓣ 092/46089;

Bike World, New Antrim Street, Castlebar, Co. Mayo;
℡ 094/25220, Ⓦ www.mayocycling.ie.

Boat cruises

Corrib Princess, Woodquay, Galway ℡ 091/592447. Ninety-minute cruises daily from Woodquay.

Killary Cruises near Leenane ℡ freephone 1800 415151,
Ⓦ www.killarycruises.com. This offers ninety-minute catamaran all-weather trips down Killary fjord.

Island Ferries Victoria Place, Galway ℡ 091/568093;
Ⓦ www.aranislandferries.com. Trips from Rossaveel to Inishmore (2–4 daily; 35min), Inisheer (1–2 daily; 60min) and Inishmaan (1–2 daily; 50min). Singles are €10, returns €19 with coach connections to and from Galway.

Portumna Passenger Boat Company Portumna, Co. Galway
℡ 086/391 8364. Hour-long cruises of Lough Derg (June–Aug) and trips to Terryglass on the Tipperary side of the water (April, May, early Sept).

Truelight Roundstone, Co. Galway ℡ 095/21034, Ⓦ www.truelight .ie. Three-hour harbour cruises in a traditional hooker, €40.

Cinemas

Ballina Cineplex Mercy St, Ballina, Co. Mayo ℡ 096/7077,
Ⓦ www.filminfo.net.

Galway Omniplex Headford Rd, Galway city ℡ 091/567800,
Ⓦ www.filminfo.net.

Mayo Movie World Moneen, Castlebar, Co. Mayo
℡ 094/9025472, Ⓦ www.mayoleisurepoint.ie.

Westport Cineplex James St, Westport, Co. Mayo
℡ 098/24242.

Horse racing

Galway Racecourse Ballybrit, Galway city Ⓦ www
.galwayraces.com. Race meetings: July 25–31, Sept 4–6, Oct 30-31.

Ballinrobe Racecourse Ballinrobe, Co. Mayo Ⓦ www.hri.ie. Race meetings: May 4, 30–31, June 21, July 18–19, Aug 8, 28.

Roscommon Racecourse Roscommon town Ⓦ www.hri.ie.
Race meetings: May 16, June 12–13, July 4–5, Aug 2, 15, Sept 12, Oct 3.

Horse riding and pony trekking

Carrowholly Stables and Trekking Centre Carrowholly,
Westport, Co. Mayo ℡ 098/27044, Ⓦ www.carrowholly-stables .com; **Cleggan Trekking Centre** Clifden, Co. Galway

095/44746; **Drummindoo Equitation Centre** Westport, Co.
Mayo ☎ 098/25616; **Errislannan Manor** Clifden, Co. Galway
☎ 095/21134; **Laragan Stables** Clifden, Co. Galway
☎ 095/44735; **Mulrany Riding School** Newport, Co Mayo
☎ 098/36126; **Renvyle House** Renvyle, Co. Galway,
☎ 095/43511, ⓦ www.renvyle.com.

Leisure centre

Mayo Leisure Point Moneen, Castlebar, Co. Mayo
☎ 094/25473. Ireland's largest indoor entertainment park with a
cinema, rollerball, karting, video games and bowling.

Swimming

Leisureland Salthill, Galway city ☎ 091/521455. Daily year-round,
opening hours vary. Adults €7, children €4.80. This leisure complex in Salthill has a swimming pool with slides, a kiddies' pool,
pirate ship and crazy golf. Nearby in Salthill is Perk's funfair, mega
trampolines, remote-controlled boats and bungee jumping.

Westport Leisure Park Westport, Co. Mayo ☎ 098/29160.
Features a swimming pool with a kids' obstacle course.

Water sports and adventure sports

Atlantic Adventure Centre Louisburgh Rd, Westport, Co. Mayo
☎ 098/64806. Sailing courses for all.

Hodson Bay Watersport Athlone, Co. Roscommon
☎ 1890/704090, ⓦ www.hodsonbay.com. Tour Lough Ree by
powerboat.

Little Killary Adventure Centre Leenane, Co. Galway
☎ 095/43411, ⓦ www.killary.com. Day and residential courses
from rock-climbing to mountain biking, sail-boarding, archery,
kayaking and windsurfing.

Scuba Dive West Glasilaun Beach, Co. Galway ☎ 095/43922,
ⓦ www.scubadivewest.com. Courses and diving off the coast.

Surf Mayo Westport, Co. Mayo ☎ 087/621 2508. Surfing
instruction, wetsuit and surfboard hire.

Accommodation

Galway Bay Hotel Salthill, Galway city ☎ 091/520520,
ⓦ www.galwaybayhotel.net. Four-star hotel overlooking Galway
Bay, 5min from the city centre. Family rooms. Features Penguin
Kids Activity Camp for 4–12s.

Hodson Bay Hotel Athlone, Co. Roscommon ☎ 090/6442000,
ⓦ www.hodsonbayhotel.com. Picturesque location on the

shores of Lough Ree. Family rooms and interconnecting rooms. Features Penguin Kids Activity Camp for 4-12s.

Westport Woods Hotel Quay Rd, Westport, Co. Mayo ⓣ 098/25811, ⓦ www.westportwoodshotel.com. In a woodland setting 3min from Westport town centre, Go!Kids! activity programme for tots to teens. Leisure centre and swimming pool, pony trekking available. Beside Westport House and Country Park.

The Station House Hotel Clifden, Co. Galway ⓣ 095/21699, ⓣ www.clifdenstationhouse.com. Converted railway station in a courtyard setting. Located in Clifden, capital of Connemara. Family specials. Railway Kids Club. Swimming and leisure facilities

Places to eat

Ard Bia 15 Cross St, Galway ⓣ 087/236 8648, ⓦ www.ardbia.com. A great little café and coffee shop in the funky part of town with good vegetarian selections.

Dolphin Restaurant Inishbofin, Co. Galway ⓣ 095/45992. Seafood, meat and vegetarian options.

The Tavern Murrisk, Westport, Co. Mayo ⓣ 098/64060. Pub-restaurant nestling at the foot of Croagh Patrick Mountain and overlooking Clew Bay. Great early bird menu, and special kids' menu, and good food for adults too.

Two Dog Café Church Hill, Clifden, Co. Galway ⓦ www.twodogcafe.ie. Good coffee, great food – sandwiches, tortilla wraps, salads – and Internet access.

12

Sligo and Leitrim

These two counties both have luscious scenery. Sligo is known for the beautiful mountains Benbulben and Knocknarea and includes the major parts of the gorgeous Glencar and Lough Gill, as well as some marvel-

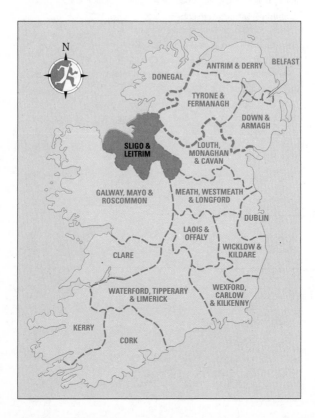

lous beaches to the west at Enniscrone and Rosses Point and to the north at Streedagh Strand. The rolling farmland of South Sligo is renowned for its traditional music. Sligo town itself is a lively, bustling, traffic-clogged place which might have plenty of amenities, but isn't the best place for families to stay.

In terms of population, Leitrim is the smallest county in Ireland, home to a mere 26,000 people. Often neglected by tourists, its northern mountains and glens and its many lakes, including the vast Lough Allen, remain largely unexploited. With its riverside setting, Carrick-on-Shannon is a popular boating centre, as well as being the county's largest town.

Sligo

Culkin's Emigration Museum

Dromore West, Co. Sligo ℡ 096/914 7152. June–Sept Mon–Sat 11am–5pm, Sun 1–5pm. Adults €3, children €2.

Daniel Culkin's Shipping and Emigration Agency operated on this spot from the nineteenth century to the 1930s and arranged for many Sligo people to leave for a better life in the USA. The museum contains the original Agency shop, depicts life in post-Famine Ireland and recounts the tales of some of those locals who emigrated, something to ponder in these days of a booming Irish economy.

Waterpoint

Pier Rd, Enniscrone, Co. Sligo ℡096/36999, Ⓦ www.waterpoint.ie. Call for opening times. Adults €7, children €4.50, infants €3.

This modern complex offers a heated swimming pool and a children's special fun pool, as well as a massive 210ft-long water slide. There are also fitness, sauna, Jacuzzi and steam-room facilities for adults and a snack bar.

Coleman Heritage Centre

Gurteen, Co. Sligo ⓣ071/918 2599,
ⓦwww.colemanirishmusic.com. Mon–Sat 10am–5pm.
Audiovisual display adults €4, children €2, family €10.

Erected in honour of Ireland's most influential traditional
fiddler, Michael Coleman (1891–1945), who hailed from
nearby Killavil, the centre offers an audiovisual display on his
life together with various interactive touchscreens supplying
information on traditional music. Best of all, however, are
the evening shows of traditional music and dance, usually by
local musicians (April–Oct Wed & Sat), a great alternative if
you want to hear some traditional sounds but don't want to
take your kids to the pub. The centre also stocks an excellent
range of CDs and books.

Gillighan's World

Knocknashee, Lavagh, Co. Sligo ⓣ071/913 0286,
ⓦwww.gillighansworld.com. May Fri–Sun noon–7pm;
June–Sept Tues–Sun 11am–7pm. Adults €7, children €6.

Knocknashee literally means "hill of the fairies", a place
with long-standing associations with the little folk, and
Gillighan's World is an imaginative attempt to enlighten and
entertain visitors about fairy life and lore. Its elegant moun-
tainside setting combines botanical gardens and miniature
villages populated by natural flora and fauna. There are
ponds and a trout lake, too, plus a pet village and play area
and, in December, the place transforms itself into "Winter
Wonderland".

Eagles Flying, Ballymote

Portinch, Ballymote, Co. Sligo ⓣ071/918 9310,
ⓦwww.eaglesflying.com. Daily Easter–Nov 10.30am–12.30pm &
2.30–4.30pm. Adults €7, children €4, family €20.

Ireland's largest sanctuary for birds of prey and various
breeds of owl offers displays daily at 11am and 3pm, where
various falcons, vultures and eagles can be observed free-flying, while younger children will enjoy the small pet zoo, featuring various farm animals plus rabbits and guinea pigs.

Sligo Folk Park

Millview House, Riverstown, Co. Sligo ⓣ071/916 5001,
ⓦwww.sligofolkpark.com. Daily May–Oct 10am–4.30pm. Adults
€5, children €3, family €14.

Aiming to offer an insight into rural life at the end of the
nineteenth century, the park's re-created village street features a forge, creamery, pub and grocery, and occasional craft
demonstrations, while the museum includes many other
artefacts and memorabilia. The park occupies the grounds of

the restored Millview House and offers a nature trail along the banks of the Unshin River.

Sligo Abbey

Abbey St, Sligo town, Co. Sligo ⓣ 071/914 6406, ⓦ www .heritageireland.ie. Mid-March to Oct daily 10am–6pm; Nov & Dec Fri–Sun 9.30am–4.30pm. Adults €2, children €1, family €5.50.

Though everyone calls it an abbey and it's on Abbey Street, these pretty, well-preserved ruins are actually those of a mid-thirteenth-century Dominican friary which served as such until the building was sacked during the rebellion of 1641. As the town's only surviving medieval building, it's well worth visiting for its many carvings, including Gothic and Renaissance tomb sculptures, elegant cloisters and fifteenth-century high altar. Tours are available on request and provide an informed insight into the life of the friars.

Carrowmore Megalithic Cemetery

Sligo town, Co. Sligo ⓣ 071/916 1534, ⓦ www.heritageireland.ie. Daily Easter–Oct 10am–6pm. Adults €2, children €1, family €5.50; Heritage Card.

The biggest cemetery of Megalithic tombs in Ireland lies some three miles from Sligo town centre off the R292 Strandhill road. So far, some sixty tombs have been located in this field and scientific analysis suggests that some may date as far back as 5400 BC, all good for bringing to life ancient man and his exploits. There's a restored cottage here which houses a small but very informative account of the site. High on a hill above is the 60ft-high Meabh's Cairn (known locally as "Maeve's Lump"), reputed to be the grave of the legendary Queen Meabh of Connaught.

Leitrim

The Cavan and Leitrim Railway

Dromod, Co. Leitrim ⓣ 071/963 8599, ⓦ www.irish-railway.com. April–Sept Mon–Fri 10am–5pm, Sun 1–5.30pm. €5 per person.

Operating from a restored station on the old Cavan and Leitrim Railway, right next to the existing Dublin-Sligo main line, enthusiasts run regular trips in fantastic old trains pulled by unusual engines, half a mile up the narrow-gauge track to Clooncolry (although there are plans to continue onwards to Mohill). At the time of writing the CLR had acquired a number of old aircraft, too, and these may soon be on display in the station yard.

Parke's Castle

Fivemile Bourne, Co. Leitrim ☎071/916 4149,
Ⓦwww.heritageireland.ie. Daily mid-March to Oct 10am–6pm.
Adults €2.75, children €1.25, family €7. Heritage Card.

This restored seventeenth-century Plantation castle is a real gem of a building, positioned in a romantic setting on the shore of Lough Gill. The Parke in its name was one Robert who employed the walls of a previous moated castle to build his own home. The previous owner, the chieftain Brian O'Rourke, was hung for high treason at Tyburn in London in 1591 for sheltering a Spaniard from the wrecked Armada. Much of the castle's structure is still in very good shape and its rooms inside, including the forge, have been tastefully restored using traditional crafts and Irish oak. Next to the castle is a sweathouse. Boat trips around the lough leave from the landing stage here daily in summer.

Glencar Waterfall

Glencar Forest, Co. Leitrim. Open access.

Situated some seven miles west of Manorhamilton, Glencar Lough is a secluded spot and something of an angler's paradise thanks to its stocks of salmon and trout. From the car park by the lough's northern shore, a pathway rises upwards to this stunning waterfall, some 50ft high and, obviously, best seen after heavy rainfall.

Swan Island Open Farm

Keeldrin, Corrawallen, near Newtown Gore, Co. Leitrim
☎049/433 3065. Daily May–Oct 11am–6pm. Call for prices.

Swan Island is beautifully situated on the shore of Garadice Lake. The farm features more than fifty species of traditional and rare breeds and such delights as a ride in a pony cart. There's a children's play area and the two-hundred-year-old Davy's Cottage, which houses a restaurant (open from 6pm). The farm also opens in December for visits from Santa. To get here, take the R199 Killeshandra road from Ballinamore to Newtowngore, then follow the Swan Island signs.

Sports and activities

Adventure centres

Lough Allen Adventure Centre Ballinagleragh, Co. Leitrim
☎071/964 3292.

Boat rental and cruises

Ballinamore Boats 3 Railway Rd, Ballinamore, Co. Leitrim
⊤071/964 4079. The *Sliabh an Iarainn Sunset* (Ireland's first wheelchair-accessible waterbus) runs daily sailings on the Shannon-Erne waterways (June–Sept daily, Oct–May Sat & Sun) and evening trips to Swan Island Open Farm for dinner and music at Davy's Cottage. Rental also available.

The Blue Lagoon Riverside, Sligo town, Co. Sligo ⊤071/914 2530. Boat rental.

The Innisfree Tour Boat Kilmore, Five Mile Bourne, Co. Leitrim ⊤071/916 4266. Operates daily sailings around Lough Gill (March–Oct) picking up passengers at Riverside in Sligo town and Parke's Castle.

Moon River Main St, Carrick-on-Shannon, Co. Leitrim ⊤071/962 1777, ⓦwww.moon-river.net. Runs 90-minute week-day afternoon trips along the Shannon during high season with extra sailings at weekends.

Cinemas

Gaiety Cinema Bridge St, Carrick-on-Shannon, Co. Leitrim ⊤071/962 1869; **Gaiety Multiplex** Wine St, Sligo town, Co. Sligo ⊤071/917 4002.

Fishing

Several boats offer fishing trips from Mullaghmore and cruises to the deserted island of Innishmurray, including **Excalibur Innishmurray Tours** ⊤087/245 0190; **Lomax Boats and Angling** ⊤071/916 6124; **Peter Power** ⊤087/257 6268; and **Gerry Sheerin** ⊤071/916 6472. Prices depend on the length of the trip and the number of people sailing.

Horse racing

Sligo Racecourse Cleveragh Rd, Sligo town ⊤071/918 3342, ⓦwww.air.ie/sligo.html. Meetings during 2005 on April 25, May 24, June 28, July 10, Aug 3, Aug 4, Aug 17. Adults €6–10, children under 14 free.

Horse riding

Co. Sligo: **Ard Chuan Equestrian Centre** Corbala ⊤096/45084; **Island View Riding Stables** Island View, Grange ⊤071/916 6156, ⓦwww.islandviewridingstables.com; **Markree Castle Riding Stables** Markree Castle, Collooney ⊤071/913 0727, ⓦwww.markreeridingstables.ie; **Sligo Riding School** Carrowmore ⊤071/916 1353; **Woodlands Equestrian Centre** Loughill, Lavagh, Tubbercurry ⊤071/918 4220.

Co. Leitrim: Drumcoura City, Ballinasloe ☏071/964 5708;
Hayden Equestrian Centre Bornacoola, Dromod ☏071/963
8049; **Moorlands Equestrian Centre** Curraghill, Drumshanbo
☏071/964 1500.

Surfing schools

Perfect Day Surf School Strandhill, Co. Sligo, ☏071/916 8464;
Seventh Wave Surf School Easky, Co. Sligo ☏096/49020.
Otherwise visit the **Surf and Information Centre** in the centre of
Easky (July & Aug daily 9.30am–5pm, Sept–June Mon–Fri
10am–2pm; ☏096/49020).

Swimming

Carrick Swimming Pool Carrick-on-Shannon, Co. Leitrim
☏071/962 1400; **Sligo Sports Complex** Cleveragh, Sligo town,
Co. Sligo ☏071/916 0539.

Accommodation

Beach Hotel and Leisure Club The Harbour, Mullaghmore,
Co. Sligo ☏071/916 6103, Ⓦwww.beachhotelmullaghmore
.com. Overlooking the Atlantic, the *Beach* has its own swimming pool and gym and is ideally set for plenty of outdoor
activities. It offers a babysitting service and a range of special
breaks.

Gortmór House Lismakeegan, Carrick-on-Shannon, Co. Leitrim
☏071/962 1439. A farmhouse B&B, a mile or so northeast of
Carrick, with a family room and its own Shetland ponies.

Millhouse Keenaghan, Ballymote, Co. Sligo ☏0918/3449,
Ⓦwww.sligo-accommodation.com. Superb B&B in a tranquil
South Sligo location with its own tennis court and award-
winning breakfasts.

The Old Rectory Fenagh, Ballinamore, Co. Leitrim ☏071/964
4089, Ⓦwww.theoldrectoryireland.com. A beautiful Georgian
house in a delightful setting – very welcoming to families; 25
percent child reductions.

Places to eat

Cryan's Bridge St, Carrick-on-Shannon, Co. Leitrim. Fine bar
serving substantial and highly popular meals.

Eithna's Seafood Restaurant The Harbour, Mullaghmore, Co.
Sligo ☏071/916 6407. Local seafood, caught by one host and

cooked by the other with organic meat and vegetarian options; open daily Easter–Nov 6.30–9.30pm.

The Gateway Bar & The Loft Restaurant Lord Edward St, Sligo town, Co. Sligo ☎071/914 6770. Downstairs is a railway-themed bar offering a daily carvery lunch while upstairs *The Loft* serves the most extensive menu in the county.

Yeats Tavern Restaurant & Davis's Pub Drumcliffe Bridge, Co. Sligo ☎071/916 3117. Family-run place dishing up Irish lamb and beef, plus local seafood such as oysters and clams.

13

Donegal

With its bluff headlands and thrilling seascapes, multitude of loughs and staggering mountains, you could easily spend two weeks in Donegal and regret that you had not planned for a longer stay. The opportunities for outdoor activities are extensive and there are sever-

For information about events visit ⓦwww.donegaldirect.ie and ⓦwww.dun-na-ngall.com or see the *Donegal Democrat* newspaper. The county's main tourist office is in Letterkenny (Ⓣ070/912 1160); and there are also seasonal offices in Buncrana (Ⓣ074/936 26000; Bundoran, (Ⓣ071/984 1350); Donegal town (Ⓣ074/972 1148); and Dungloe (Ⓣ074/952 1297).

al seaside resorts (Bundoran being the most popular), as well as plenty of places for families to visit on inclement days. However, without your own transport getting around the county is not easy, especially out of season.

Deane's Equestrian Centre and Open Farm

Darney, Bruckless, Co. Donegal Ⓣ074/973 7160,
ⓔdeanesequestrian@eircom.net. Farm: April–Aug 10am–4pm.
Horse riding: all year. Call for prices.

This long-established open farm has a variety of animals and birds on show and also offers pony rides (€3.50) and children's riding lessons (from €6 for 15min to €14 for 1hr), as well as trekking for more advanced riders (children must be aged 10 or over).

Ards Forest Park

Ards, Co. Donegal Ⓣ074/912 1139. Daily: April–Sept
10am–9pm; Oct–March 10am–4.30pm. Free.

Situated on the N56 between Creeslough and Dunfanaghy, this twelve-hundred acre park provides plenty of scope for a family outing. Its varied terrain comprises sandy beaches, rivers and woodland and there are several waymarked nature and walking trails plus picnic and play areas. The park is home to a wide variety of bird life, as well as a herd of red deer, and rarely gets crowded thanks to its car-parking limit of two hundred vehicles.

Grianán Ailigh

Burt, Co. Donegal. Daily dawn–dusk. Free.

Set a steep mile up a hill above the village of Burt, the Grianán Ailigh dates back to around 1700 BC and is a remarkable circular fort, prominent enough in the past to have been included in Ptolemy's second-century AD map of the world, and the base for various northern Irish chieftains. However, by the nineteenth century much of its stone had been carried away and it was reconstructed by an archaeologist from Derry in the 1870s. The views of Inishowen, the loughs and other parts of the Donegal countryside from here are simply stunning. Back in Burt, the Grianán Ailigh Centre (daily: June & Aug 10am–7pm; Sept–May noon–4.30pm; €5 per person; ℡074/936 8000, ⓦ www .griananailigh.ie) lays on an exhilarating audiovisual account of the fort's history and a return minibus trip (handy for those without transport).

Millbridge Open Farm

Convoy, Co. Donegal ℡ 074/914 7125. July & Aug Tues–Sat 11am–5pm, Sun 1.30–5pm. Adults €5, children €3.

There's all manner of farm animals here to meet and touch, plus wagon rides, an adventure play area and the opportunity to paddle a canoe or row a boat (activities cost an additional €1–1.75 per person).

Doagh Visitor Centre

Doagh Island, Inishowen, Co. Donegal ℡ 074/937 8078. Daily Easter–Oct 10am–5.30pm. €5 per person.

Through buildings such as a fairy house and a re-created farm cottage plus various tableaux, the centre provides a wealth of information on local customs while its Famine Walk offers a challenging account of the effects of the Great Hunger and draws parallels with the present-day situation in Africa. From late November until Christmas it transforms itself into "Donegal's Lapland" complete with a Christmas show, reindeer, an elves' kingdom and, of course, Santa (nightly 5pm; adults €7, children €14 including present from Santa).

Donegal Bay Waterbus

The Quay, Donegal town ℡ 074/972 3666, ⓦ www.donegalbaywaterbus.com. Easter–Sept daily, weather permitting – call for times. Adults €10, children €5, family tickets available on request.

The waterbus takes you on a ten-mile trip around Donegal Bay, lasting just over an hour, and passing such sites as the old Abbey, the burial place of the chieftain Red Hugh O'Donnell and the ruins of O'Boyle Castle. It also sails past oyster- and mussel-beds and offers the chance to view plenty of bird life and a colony of seals.

Donegal Castle

Tirconnaill St, Donegal town ℡ 01/074 972 2405, ⓦ www .heritageireland.ie. Mid-March to Oct daily 10am–6pm; Nov & Dec Fri–Sun 9.30am–4.30pm. Adults €3.50, children €1.25, family €8.25. Heritage Card.

Donegal Castle can trace its origins to a tower house constructed by the Gaelic chieftain Red Hugh O'Donnell in the fifteenth century, but was rebuilt and extended by Sir Basil Brooke who was given command of the town after the English defeat of the second Red Hugh in 1603. Various displays recount the castle's history, but the real enjoyment lies in taking a guided tour of its richly furnished rooms, some hung with French tapestries, and marvelling at the building's combination of strong defence and domestic splendour.

Donegal Railway Heritage Centre

Old Station House, Tirconnaill St, Donegal town ☏ 074/972 2655, ⓦ www.countydonegalrailway.com. Mon–Fri 10am–5pm, Sat 11am–5pm, Sun 2–5pm. Adults €3.50, children €2, family €10.

The Heritage Centre is devoted to recapturing the delights of the old narrow-gauge Donegal County Railway (or "Wee Donegal" as it was affectionately known) which ran all the way from Derry to Ballyshannon for a hundred years until 1959. The centre has photo displays, models and railway artefacts, and a simulator lets you imagine driving a steam train through the Barnesmore Gap. It also has a working model railway and enthusiasts are busy restoring old rolling stock in the yard.

The Workhouse

Dunfanaghy, Co. Donegal ☏ 074/913 6540. Mon–Fri 10am–5pm, Sat & Sun noon–5pm. Adults €4, children €2.

Dunfanaghy's workhouse was built in 1845 just before the outbreak of the Great Famine. However, as the hunger took its toll, by 1847 it was housing over six hundred people. The story of one local inmate, "Wee" Hannah Herrity, is recounted upstairs through a series of tableaux each with its own commentary. Downstairs houses a coffee shop, an art gallery displaying temporary exhibitions and a craft and book shop.

Beaches

Donegal's coastline includes a number of startlingly good beaches, with miles of golden sand. However, be advised that some are not suitable for swimming because of changing tides and strong undercurrents, and bring your own picnic as few of the most enjoyable ones are near catering facilities. Amongst the best are: Tullan Strand, Buncrana; Rossnowlagh; Murvagh (near Donegal town); Maghery (look out for the Assarancagh Waterfall on the way from Ardara); Narin (where you can walk out to Inniskeel Island at low tide); Magheraroarty; Falcarragh; and, on the Inishowen Peninsula, Tullagh Strand, Pollan Strand, Culdaff and Kinnego Bay.

Fort Dunree Military Museum

Dunree, Inishowen, Co. Donegal ☎074/936 1817,
Ⓦwww.dunree.pro.ie. June–Sept Mon–Sat 10.30am–6pm, Sun
1–6pm; Oct–May Mon–Fri 10.30am–4.30pm, Sat & Sun 1–6pm.
Adults €4, children €2.

Fort Dunree began life as a Martello tower during the
Napoleonic Wars and was erected very near the spot where
one of the leaders of the 1798 Rebellion, Wolfe Tone, was
brought ashore. The fort was extensively enlarged during the
late nineteenth century and nowadays houses a collection of
military memorabilia, somewhat enlivened by interactive
displays. The old fort hospital now holds an exhibition
devoted to local wildlife and their habitats.

Father McDyer's Folk Village Museum

Glencolmcille, Co. Donegal ☎074/973 0017,
Ⓦwww.glenfolkvillage.com. Easter–Sept Mon–Sat 10am–6pm,
Sun noon–6pm. Adults €2.75, children €2, family €9.50.

Named in honour of a priest who helped to catalyse an eco-
nomic revival in the area during the 1950s, this museum
consists of a cluster of replica thatched buildings furnished
according to the fashions of the 1700s, 1800s and early
1900s, and offering the chance to see how our ancestors
might have lived. The reception building features displays of
the area's history and heritage and there's also a replica of a
National School and a shebeen house where you can enjoy
delights such as seaweed wine. There's also a teahouse here
with its own bakery and a craft shop (oh, and the beach is
just over the dunes by the edge of the car park).

St Connell's Museum and Heritage Centre

Glenties, Co. Donegal ☎074/955 1227. June–Sept Mon–Sat
10am–1pm, Sun 2–4.30pm. Adults €2.50, children €1.

Occupying the old Courthouse, this small museum packs a
host of information into every available space. Inside you'll
find displays on local wildlife, music, antiquities, Donegal
railways, household artefacts, antique toys and the effects of
the Great Famine, including a famine pot from the Glenties
workhouse. The basement houses the building's former cells,
as well as re-creations of a schoolroom, kitchen and forge.

Inishowen Maritime Museum and Planetarium

Old Coastguard Station, Greencastle, Co. Donegal ☎074/938
1363, Ⓦwww.inishowenmaritime.com. Easter–Sept Mon–Sat
10am–6pm, Sun noon–6pm; Oct–Easter Mon–Fri 10am–5pm.
Museum: adults €4, children €2, family €10; museum &
planetarium: adults €8, children €4, family €20.

If you love boats and the sea, you'll thoroughly enjoy the range of exhibits housed in the Maritime Museum, ranging from memorabilia and ancient seafaring equipment to a fully-rigged "Greencastle yawl" (a traditional fishing boat) to a wildfowling punt with a swivel gun and a nineteenth-century rocket-driven cart. The planetarium allows visitors to view the stars on any historical date and see how the skies have changed over the last two thousand years. Lastly, there are special Laser Light concerts on various summer evenings, featuring a thrilling and dynamic laser system linked to a wide range of music, from traditional to Led Zeppelin.

Ionad Cois Locha/The Dunlewey Lakeside Centre

Dunlewey Lough, Gweedore, Co. Donegal ⓣ 074/953 1699, ⓦ www.dunleweycentre.com. Easter–Oct Mon–Sat 10.30am–6pm, Sun 11–6pm. Cottage tour or boat trip: adults €5, children €3.50, family €12.50; combined cottage tour and boat trip: adults €8, children €6, family €20; adventure play area: adults €3.50, children €3, family €10.

Right next to the stunningly beautiful Dunlewey Lough, this centre incorporates a craft, book and CD shop as well as a popular restaurant. Outside there are restored farm buildings, including a farm museum and plenty of more recently arrived farm animals, together with a re-creation of the home of a local weaver. The adventure play area has its own artificial lake and also activities under cover for rainy days, but best of all is the boat trip on the Lough complete with storyteller. The centre also hosts the Trad Trathnóna series of traditional music concerts on Tuesday evenings and occasional other nights during the summer months.

Glenveagh National Park and Castle

Churchill, Letterkenny, Co. Donegal ⓣ 074/913 7090, ⓦ www.heritageireland.ie. Daily, mid-March to early Nov 10am–6.30pm. Park: adults €2.75, children €1.25, family €7; castle: adults €2.75, children €1.25, family €7. Heritage Card.

Entered via the R251, several miles north of Churchill, the National Park incorporates much of the Derryveagh Mountains. It's splendid walking country but it's the castle, overlooking Lough Beagh, which attracts most visitors. The park's visitor centre provides very detailed, interactive displays on local wildlife and geology and, from here, there's a free minibus ride along the lough shore to the castle itself. Before taking the guided tour be sure to climb through the gardens to absorb the fabulous view of the lough and surrounding countryside.

Jungleking

Oldtown, Letterkenny, Co. Donegal ℡074/917 7731,
ⓦwww.jungleking.ie. Daily 10am–7pm. €6.

A purpose-built, jungle-themed play area with activities for children under 12, including snake slides, activity towers and a soft play area.

Letterkenny Karting Centre

Ballymaleel, Letterkenny, Co. Donegal ℡074/912 9077.
Mon–Sat 1–10.30pm. From €10 for a 10min ride.

Take a kart for a spin on a track more than 900yd long, race against others (the track can cater for twenty competitors at one time) or just practise your skills.

Newmills Corn and Flax Mills

Churchill Rd, Newmills, Co. Donegal ℡074/912 5115, ⓦwww
.heritageireland.ie. Daily mid-June to Sept 10am–6.30pm. Adults
€2.50, children €1.20, family €6.30. Heritage Card.

The oldest building in this complex of mills dates back some four hundred years and it was only as recently as 1982 that the mills stopped operating commercially. Fortunately, much of the machinery is still in use and there's the chance to watch it in operation, powered by the River Swilly turning a massive water wheel, one of the largest in Ireland.

The Old Courthouse

The Diamond, Lifford, Co. Donegal ℡074/914 1733,
ⓦwww.infowing.ie/seatofpower. Mon–Fri 9am–5pm, Sat
10am–5pm, Sun 11.30–4pm. Adults €5, children €3, family
€12.50.

Visiting this prestigious old building, which dates back to 1746, you'll find yourself witnessing enjoyable re-enactments of famous trials (including that of the 1798 rebel Napper Tandy) before being whisked down to the original dungeons where you'll be taken into custody, charged and fingerprinted. Fortunately you can avoid a lengthy incarceration and visit the onsite restaurant to consume more pleasant fare than the typical penal diet.

Doon Fort

Narin, Co. Donegal. Open access.

This astonishing fortress occupies all of an oval-shaped islet in the middle of Lough Doon. Though some of its ancient walls are crumbling, most still stand at 15ft and 12ft thick and the inner passages were used to stash poteen in the 1950s. Getting to this tranquil setting can be difficult, but, driving from Ardara to Narin, turn left at the Rosbeg-

Tramore Beach signpost a mile before Narin, then next head right up the lane shortly after the school. After a few hundred yards you'll spot a "boat rental" sign pointing down to a farmhouse where you can rent a rowing boat for €3, taking you into a "Famous Five"-type adventure that all the family should enjoy.

Flight of the Earls Heritage Centre

Rathmullan, Co. Donegal ☎074/915 8131,
Ⓦwww.flightoftheearls.com. June–Sept Mon–Sat 10am–6pm, Sun 12.30–6pm; Oct–May Mon–Sat 10am–1pm & 2–5pm, Sun 11am–3pm. Adults €5, children €2.

Housed in a fort built by the British in 1810 as defence against a feared French invasion, the loughside centre focuses on the 1607 Flight of the Earls (a key moment in Irish history) and, particularly, the O'Donnell and O'Neill chieftains. Displays and exhibits set the flight's historical background and explain the Plantation of Ulster, describing the exploits of prominent local families and incorporating hanging fabrics to re-create the atmosphere of sixteenth-century Gaelic court life. Those who want to see the exact spot from which the earls are believed to have departed should head to the slipway at Portnamurry, three-quarters of a mile towards Ramelton.

Leisureland

Redcastle, Co. Donegal ☎074/938 2306,
Ⓦwww.leisurelandredcastle.ie. March–May & Sept–Oct Sat & Sun noon–7.30pm; June–Aug daily noon–6pm. Charges for various amusements.

Situated off the R238 Muff–Moville road, Leisureland is an indoor amusement centre offering a range of rides and activities for ages 3–14. Amongst the attractions are a pirate ship, safari train, eight-ball pool and carousel, or you can test your driving skills out on the dodgems and F1 cars and beat opponents at air hockey. All activities are supervised and there's also a fast-food restaurant.

Slieve League

Bunglass, Teelin, Co. Donegal. Open access.

Reckoned to be the tallest of their kind in Europe, the marine cliffs of Slieve League are one of the most thrilling sights in the whole country. To get there, follow the signs out of Teelin to the car park at Bunglass and be warned that the road takes you along sharp bends and up vertiginous inclines. At Bunglass you can view the two-thousand-foot cliff face in all its glory, its mineral deposits sparkling in the sun as the sea crashes below. Older children can take the path up to the cliff top for a spectacular view of the waters below and, on a good day, up to a third of Ireland. Another way of viewing the cliffs is to take a boat trip from Teelin on the Nuala Star (℡ 074/973 9365, ⓦ www.nwcsa.com /nualasta; call for times and prices).

Sports and activities

Adventure and activity centres

Donegal Adventure Centre Dinglei Coush, Bundoran ℡ 071/984 2418, ⓦ www.donegal-holidays.com; **Gartan Outdoor Education Centre** Churchill, Letterkenny ℡ 074/913 7032, ⓦ www.gartan.com; **Irishadventure.com** Hillhead, Ardara ℡ 074/954 1100/℡ 1890 210 571, ⓦ www.irishadventure.com; **Malinmore Adventure Centre** Malinmore ℡ 074/973 0006.

Bicycle rental

Bikes and Toys Carndonagh ℡ 074/937 4084; **Don Byrne** West End, Ardara ℡ 074/954 1658; **Hire and Sell** Bundoran ℡ 071/984 1526; **O'Doherty's** Main St, Donegal town ℡ 074/972 1119.

Cinemas

The Abbey Centre Market St, Ballyshannon ℡ 071/985 1375, ⓦ www.abbeycentre.net; **Bundoran Cineplex** Station Rd, Bundoran ℡ 071/982 9999, ⓦ www.cineplexbundoran.com; **Century Cinemas** Leckview Lane, Pearse Rd, Letterkenny ℡ 074/912 5050, ⓦ www.letterkennycinema.net; **Lifford Strabane Cineplex** Lifford ℡ 074/914 1963, ⓦ www .liffordstrabane.com.

Horse riding

Ashtree Stables Coole, Cranford ℡ 074/915 3312; **Carrigart Riding Centre** Wood Quarter, Cranford ℡ 074/915 3583; **Dunfanaghy Riding Stables** *Arnolds Hotel*, Dunfanaghy ℡ 074/913 6208, ⓦ www.arnoldshotel.com; **Golden Sands Equestrian Centre** Rathmullan ℡ 074/915 8124; **Homefield Equestrian Centre** Bayview Ave, West End, Bundoran ℡ 071/984 1288; **Inch Island Stables** Inch Island, Burnfoot ℡ 074/936 0335; **Lenamore Stables**, Muff ℡ 074/938 4022, ⓦ www.lenamorestables.com.

Pitch and putt

Pin Tavern Pitch and Putt Drumnahoe, Letterkenny ℡ 074/912 5688; **Sandfield Pitch and Putt** Narin Rd, Ardara ℡ 074/954 1344.

Swimming

Waterworld Seafront, Bundoran ☎071/984 1172,
Ⓦwww.waterworldbundoran.com. Easter week, May & Sept Sat
& Sun, June–Aug daily 10am–7pm. Adults €7.50, children under
8 €5, under 3 €3. This massively popular indoor complex features two leisure pools, flumes, a wave pool with rapids and,
most thrilling of all, the ultra-speedy "whizzer" slide. Also here
are the Aqua Maris seaweed baths which offer adults the
chance to wallow in the invigorating green "soup".

Accommodation

Lakeside Centre Caravan and Camping Park Ballyshannon
☎071/985 2822. An ideal location for your holiday, or as a base
from which to explore the northwest.
Highlands Hotel Glenties ☎074/955 1111, Ⓦwww
.highlandshotel.com. Family-run and family-welcoming, the
Highland is a very comfortable establishment, offering superb-
value bar and à la carte meals; child reductions.
Shandon Hotel and Leisure Centre Marble Hill Strand,
Sheephaven Bay, Dunfanaghy ☎074/913 6317, Ⓦwww
.shandonhotel.com. Not so much a very relaxing hotel, but a
child-friendly entertainment centre, featuring swimming pool,
basketball court and indoor play area.
Trean House Tremone, Lecamy ☎074/916 7121, Ⓦwww
.treanhouse.com This very comfortable seaside farmhouse B&B
is an enjoyable base for exploring Inishowen.

Places to eat

An Chiston Restaurant Glencolmcille ☎074/973 0213. Open
9am till 9.30pm for a variey of homecooked Irish food.
Blueberry Tearoom and Restaurant Castle St, The Diamond,
Donegal town ☎074/972 2933. A cosy place which serves
lunches, snacks and desserts.
Leo's Tavern Meenaleck. Home pub of the band Clannad, *Leo's*
is a very popular place for families, not least for its superb fish
and chips.
Sweeny's White Horse Bundoran Rd, Ballyshannon. Excellent
bar with an imaginative menu.
The Water's Edge Rathmullan ☎074/915 8182. This loughside
restaurant's range of cuisine is really hard to beat and certainly
the place to come for a treat.

14

Belfast

A s Northern Ireland's largest city, Belfast will be remembered as the focus of the continuing political disputes which have dominated so many people's lives since 1969. However, this one-time centre of shipbuilding and the linen trade is remarkably changed. The security

presence is virtually invisible, making it a very safe place for tourists, and the city's docklands and other areas have witnessed extensive reinvigoration. There are plenty of things for families to see and do here and Belfast's arts and nightlife are as good as you'll find in any major European city.

Aunt Sandra's Candy Factory

60 Castlereagh Rd ☎ 028/9073 2868, Ⓦ www.irishcandyfactory .com. Mon–Fri 9.30am–5pm, Sat 10am–4pm. Free (advance booking essential).

A re-creation of the original 1953 shop, complete with wooden ceilings and slate floors, Aunt Sandra's offers visitors the chance to watch the handmade manufacture of a range of chocolates and candies and to sample delights such as humbugs and traditional fudge.

Belfast Zoo

Off Antrim Rd ☎ 028/9077 6277, Ⓦ www.belfastzoo.co.uk. Daily: April–Sept 10am–5pm; Oct–March 10am–2.30pm. April–Sept adults £6.70, children £3.40, family £18.40; Oct–March adults £5.70, children £2.80, family £15.20.

Spread over landscaped parkland, the zoo houses more than one hundred and sixty species of rare and endangered animals and focuses firmly upon conservation and education. There's a host of monkeys, plenty of big cats, lemurs, giraffes, tapirs and sea lions, alongside many wildfowl and a walk-through aviary, but the biggest draw is probably the meerkats who live in the African enclosure.

Cave Hill Country Park and Belfast Castle

Antrim Rd. Daily dawn–dusk. Free.

Cave Hill dominates the Belfast skyline north of the city and takes its name from the Neolithic caves which puncture its

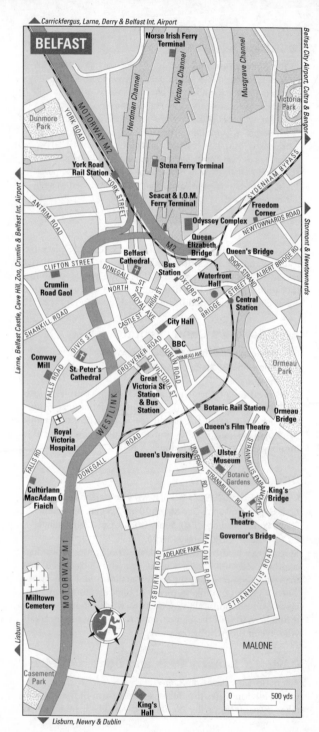

▲ Carrickfergus, Larne, Derry & Belfast Int. Airport

BELFAST

Belfast City Airport, Cultra & Bangor

Norse Irish Ferry Terminal

Herdman Channel

Victoria Channel

Musgrave Channel

Victoria Park

Dunmore Park

YORK ROAD

MOTORWAY M2

York Road Rail Station

YORK STREET

Stena Ferry Terminal

SYDENHAM BYPASS

ANTRIM ROAD

Seacat & I.O.M. Ferry Terminal

Freedom Corner

Stormont & Newtownards

Odyssey Complex

NEWTOWNARDS ROAD

M2

Queen Elizabeth Bridge

Queen's Bridge

CLIFTON STREET

Belfast Cathedral

DONEGALL ST

Bus Station

OXFORD ST

Waterfront Hall

SHORT STRAND

ALBERT BRIDGE RD

Crumlin Road Gaol

NORTH ST

ROYAL AVE

HIGH ST

BRIDGE STREET

Central Station

SHANKILL ROAD

Larne, Belfast Castle, Cave Hill, Zoo, Crumlin & Belfast Int. Airport

CASTLE ST

City Hall

Conway Mill

DIVIS ST

GROSVENER ROAD

GT. VICTORIA ST

DUBLIN ROAD

BBC

ORMEAU AVE

Ormeau Park

FALLS ROAD

St. Peter's Cathedral

Great Victoria St Station & Bus Station

WESTLINK

DONEGALL

ROAD

Botanic Rail Station

Ormeau Bridge

FALLS RD

Royal Victoria Hospital

Queen's Film Theatre

STRANMILLIS ROAD

Queen's University

UNIVERSITY

Ulster Museum

Botanic Gardens

STRANMILLIS RD

STRANMILLIS EMBANKMENT

King's Bridge

Cultúrlann MacAdam O Fiaich

Lyric Theatre

Governor's Bridge

LISBURN ROAD

ADELAIDE PARK

MALONE ROAD

STRANMILLIS ROAD

MOTORWAY M1

Milltown Cemetery

N

Lisburn

MALONE

Casement Park

0   500 yds

King's Hall

▼ Lisburn, Newry & Dublin

cliffs. The hill acquired the nickname "Napoleon's Nose" in the nineteenth century because of its resemblance to the Emperor of France's physiognomy. The park is a haven for many forms of wildlife and a hunting ground, too, for birds of prey such as kestrels. There are also three waymarked trails, the longest of which (at 4 miles) passes the caves on the way to the viewpoint of McArt's Fort, while the shortest passes the Adventurous Playground (suitable for 3- to 14-year-olds, ☎028/9037 1013 for opening times and prices) and the Millennium Maze (free). In the centre of the park stands Belfast Castle which houses the Cave Hill Visitor Centre (Mon–Sat 9am–10.30pm, Sun 9am–6pm; free; ☎028/9077 6925, ⓦ www.belfastcastle.co.uk) which recounts the history of the area from the Stone Age to modern times. The park also houses Belfast Zoo (see above).

Colin Glen Forest Park

Stewartstown Rd ☎028/9061 4115, ⓦ www.colinglentrust.org. Daily dawn–dusk. Free.

Five miles west of the city centre, the forest park consists of 200 acres of mixed woodland and grassland set around an attractive river glen. In addition to its waterfalls and ponds, the park provides a programme of guided walks during the summer months (including a Bluebell Walk and the fossil-collecting Dinosaur Walk) plus an environmental week in August and Bat Nights (hunts for the flying mammals in the forest). Activities usually cost £2 for adults and £1 for children and all children must be accompanied.

Lagan Lookout Centre

Donegall Quay ☎028/9031 5444, ⓦ www.laganside.com. April–Sept Mon–Fri 11am–5pm, Sat noon–5pm, Sun 2–5pm; Oct–March Tues–Fri 11am–3.30pm, Sat 1–4.30pm, Sun 2–4.30pm. Adults £1.50, children £0.75, family £4.

Designed to protect Belfast from flooding, the Lagan weir was the first completed component of the continuing river and docks redevelopment project. The raised, circular Lookout Centre explains the details of the weir project and explores the river's vital role in the development of such diverse industries as linen, rope-making and shipbuilding. Carefully positioned windows around the centre point out Belfast landmarks.

Lagan Valley Regional Park

South Belfast to Lisburn ☎028/9049 1922. Mostly open access. Free.

The Regional Park is actually a connected network of urban and countryside parks, heritage sites, nature reserves and riverside trails, extending for 11 miles along both sides of the

River Lagan between the south Belfast suburb of Stranmillis and the Upper Locks at Lisburn, Co. Antrim. Its attractions include nineteenth-century Malone House, Upper Malone Rd (Mon–Sat 10am–4.30pm; free; ☎028/9068 1246, Ⓦwww.malonehouse.co.uk), set in exquisite parkland (daily dawn–dusk) which has a fine restaurant and an art gallery occasionally featuring exhibitions of interest to children. Further south, past Shaw's Bridge, is the Giant's Ring (daily dawn–dusk; free), a massive prehistoric earthwork over 200yd in diameter, which has a dolmen at its centre.

The Regional Park's events programme runs from April to October and includes activities such as the "pond dip" (exploring life in freshwater ponds), guided rambles, discovery mornings and the butterfly discovery trail. All activities are free, but advance booking is essential for the majority.

Sheridan IMAX Cinema

Odyssey Pavilion, 2 Queen's Quay ☎028/9046 7000 for times of shows, Ⓦwww.belfastimax.com. Adults £5, children £4.

Featuring a screen ten times larger than a normal cinema (and taller than four double-decker buses stacked on top of each other) and a 12,000 watt digital surround-sound system, the cinema offers two-dimensional, large-format and 3-D screenings. Films include the ocean-exploring *Into the Deep*, the mountain-climbing *Everest, T-Rex: Back to the Crustaceans* and the *Blue Planet*, which views earth from space.

Streamvale Open Farm

38 Ballyhanwood Rd, Gilnahirk ☎028/9048 3244, Ⓦwww.streamvale.com. April–June Sat 2–6pm; July–Aug Mon–Sat 10.30am–6pm, Sun 2–6pm. Adults £3.95, children £3.50, family £14.50.

Situated off Old Dundonald Road in East Belfast (just past the International Ice Bowl, see p.130), this family-run working dairy farm offers children the chance to take part in animal feeding, pony and tractor rides, visits to the milking parlour, a mouse farm and a nature trail.

The Ulster Museum

Stranmillis Rd ☎028/9038 3000, Ⓦwww.ulstermuseum.org. Mon–Fri 10am–5pm, Sat 1–5pm, Sun 2–5pm. Free.

Much of the museum's massive collection has been displayed with children in mind and there's plenty here to entice and enjoy. The ground floor houses both a gallery of replica dinosaur skeletons and fully operational monsters from the age of industrialization, including a massive vertical steam engine, a loom and water wheels. Upstairs there's a fascinating "Made in Belfast" exhibition examining the wide productive range of the city's industries, and the hugely enjoyable Early Ireland gallery which traces the development of the prehistoric population. The museum has an excellent café and runs a "Back Pack Trail" on the last Sunday of every month (except Dec) providing free activity packs containing exercises and activities colour-coded to suit different ages.

Whowhatwherewhenwhy (W5)

Odyssey Pavilion, 2 Queen's Quay ℡ 028/9046 7700, ⓦ www.w5online.co.uk. Mon–Sat 10am–5pm, Sun noon–6pm. Adults £6, children £3.50, family £17.

Known as W5, this huge and vastly entertaining interactive scientific discovery centre is one of Belfast's most popular attractions and has almost 150 different exhibits crammed into five areas – WOW, START, GO, SEE and DO. Activities range from creating your own animated cartoon to operating a lie detector via testing your compositional skills on a laser harp. The centre operates an extensive programme of additional events and activities, especially during the school holidays, featuring regularly changing exhibitions and live science demonstrations, and now also houses an excellent photographic gallery.

Sports and activities

Bicycle rental

Life Cycles 36–37 Smithfield Market ℡ 028/9043 9959, ⓦ www.lifecycles.co.uk.

Boat trips

The Lagan Boat Company ℡ 028/9024 6609, ⓦ www.lagan-boatcompany.com. Call for times. Adults £5, children £4 per tour. Operates a 75-minute cruise down the river from the Lagan Lookout Centre to Cutter's Wharf, Stranmillis and a one-hour *Titanic Tour* around the docks from the landing stage opposite the Royal Mail building (also picking up passengers at the jetty by Odyssey Pavilion).

Cinemas

Belfast Cineplex Kennedy Centre, Falls Rd ℡ 028/9060 0988; **Movie House**, Yorkgate ℡ 028/9075 5000, ⓦ www.moviehouse.co.uk; **UGC**, Dublin Rd ℡ 0870/155 5176, ⓦ www.ugccinemas.co.uk; **Warner Village**, Odyssey Pavilion ℡ 0870/240 6020, ⓦ www.warnervillage.co.uk.

Gaelic football, hurling and camogie

Matches take place on Sunday afternoons at Casement Park, Andersonstown (☎ 028/9038 3815 for details).

Ice skating

Old Dundonald Rd Ⓦ www.theicebowl.com.

Swimming

Grove Leisure Centre York Rd ☎ 028/9035 1599; **Olympia Leisure Centre** Boucher Rd ☎ 028/9023 3369; **Shankill Leisure Centre** Shankill Rd ☎ 028/9024 1434.

Ten-pin bowling

Odyssey Bowl Odyssey Pavilion, 2 Queen's Quay ☎ 028/9046 7030, Ⓦ www.euphoriabelfast.com.

Accommodation

Greenwood Guest House 25 Park Rd ☎ 028/9020 2525, Ⓦ www.greenwoodguesthouse.com. Pleasant, family-run B&B situated next to Ormeau Park, offering bright and airy rooms and reductions for children sharing.

Holiday Inn Ormeau Ave ☎ 0870/400 9005, Ⓦ www .belfast.holiday-inn.com. Modern hotel offering stunning rooms and breakfasts and great family deals (under 12s free).

Jurys Inn Belfast Fisherwick Place, Great Victoria St ☎ 028/9053 3500, Ⓦ www.jurysdoyle.com. Offers a prime city-centre location and an all-in room-rate.

Malone Lodge Hotel 60 Eglantine Ave ☎ 028/9038 8000, Ⓦ www.malonelodgehotel.com. Very comfortable hotel near the university, offering well-equipped rooms and economy weekend breaks with reductions for children sharing.

Places to eat

Hard Rock Café Odyssey Pavilion, 2 Queen's Quay ☎ 028/9076 6990. Extensive American-style menu and walls bedecked with assorted rock music memorabilia. Daily noon–late.

Maggie May's 45 Botanic Ave ☎ 028/9032 2662. Wholesome Irish cooking served with plenty of vegetarian choices. Daily 7.45am–11pm.

The Morning Star 17–19 Pottinger's Entry. Old coaching inn, serving a splendid help-yourself lunchtime buffet and a more extensive à la carte menu upstairs.

Villa Italia 37–41 University Rd ☎028/9032 8356. Long-standing and ever-popular Italian restaurant, specializing in pasta, pizza and grills. Mon–Fri 5–11.30pm, Sat 4–11.30pm, Sun 4–10pm.

15

Antrim and Derry

A ntrim is the Northern Irish county most visited by tourists. Its splendid coast road from Larne heads northwards alongside the celebrated nine Glens of Antrim, taking in marvellous sea views on the way to Cushendall and Ballycastle before passing two major attrac-

Information

Tourist Offices in Co. Antrim include: Antrim ⓣ 028/9442 8331; Ballycastle ⓣ 028/2076 2024; Ballymena ⓣ 028/2563 8494; Carrickfergus ⓣ 028/9336 6455; Giant's Causeway ⓣ 028/ 2073 1855; Larne (ⓣ 028/9266 0038; and Portrush ⓣ 028/7082 3333. Those in Co. Derry are: Coleraine ⓣ 028/7034 4723; Derry ⓣ 028/7126 7284; Limavady ⓣ 028/7776 0307; and Magherafelt ⓣ 028/7963 1510. Useful Internet addresses for Co. Antrim include ⓦ www.carrickfergus.org, ⓦ www .causewaycoastandglens.com, ⓦ www.larne.gov.uk, ⓦ www .ballymena.gov.uk, and for Co. Derry, ⓦ www.derryvisitor.com, ⓦ www.colerainebc.gov.uk and ⓦ www.moyle-council.org.

tions, the Carrick-a-Rede rope bridge and the Giant's Causeway, and reaching the lively seaside resort of Portrush. Derry city is the main magnet in the county of the same name, a bustling place with an ever-lively arts scene.

Antrim

Brookhall Historical Farm

2 Horse Park, Ballinderry, Co. Antrim ⓣ 028/9262 1712, ⓦ www.brookhall.com. Easter–Oct Wed–Sat 11am–5pm, Sun 2–6pm. Adults £2, children £1.

Some four miles west of Lisburn, this attractive open farm features plenty of rare breeds, a duck pond, pleasant gardens and a farming museum devoted to a collection of bygone agricultural equipment.

Carrick-a-Rede Rope Bridge

Ballintoy, Co. Antrim ⓣ 028/2073 1159, ⓦ www.ntni.org.uk. Mid-March to June & Sept 10am–6pm; July–Aug 10am–7pm. Adults £2, children £1. National Trust.

Take a walk from the mainland across this swinging, bouncing sixty-foot rope bridge (guaranteed to raise whoops and screams from the bravest souls) crossing an almost 80ft-deep chasm to Carrick-a-Rede which means literally "the rock in the road", a very popular spot for salmon fishing. The rope bridge is a mile from the car park along a cliff path and is open only when weather conditions are safe.

Watertop Open Farm

188 Cushendall Rd, near Ballypatrick Forest Park, Co. Antrim

BALLINDERRY • BALLINTOY • BALLYCASTLE

@028/2076 2576, @www.ardclinis.com/Watertop. Daily
July–Aug 11am–5.30pm. Adults £2, children £1.
Some five miles southeast of Ballycastle on the A2, Watertop
offers farm tours, including the chance to watch a demon-
stration of shearing, and activities such as pony trekking,
fishing and boating (all at extra charge), as well as scenic
walks. There's a restaurant, too, and a pleasant campsite (open
April–Oct).

ECOS Millennium Environmental Centre

Kernohans Lane, Broughshane Rd, Ballymena, Co. Antrim
@028/2566 4400, @www.ecoscentre.com. Easter–Sept
Mon–Sat 10.30am–5pm, Sun noon–5pm; Oct–Easter Mon–Sat
noon–4pm. Adults £4, children £3 (under 4s free), family £12.50.
ECOS is a recently constructed centre, set in a 150-acre
park, which successfully educates on environmental issues
through a variety of entertaining and participatory activities.
Indoors, children can build their own simulations of rain-
forests, watch the speed at which a car generates its own
weight in CO_2 and learn how to reduce waste and reuse
and recycle what remains. Outside, the park houses a host of
butterflies, dragonflies, birds and wild flowers. The centre
organizes regular events such as pond-dipping and guided
rambles and runs Saturday and Sunday afternoon workshops
on a variety of enjoyable topics.

Leslie Hill Open Farm

Macfin Rd, Ballymoney, Co. Antrim @028/2766 6803.
Easter–May, Sun 2–6pm; June, Sat & Sun 2–6pm; July & Aug,
Mon–Sat 11–6pm, Sun 2–6pm. Adults £2.90, children £1.90,
family £8.50.
Home to ten generations of the Leslie family, the farm provides the chance to explore buildings, machinery, carriages
and carts and to meet a friendly collection of birds and animals, including a herd of red deer. There's also a pleasant
walled garden, walks through wooded parkland, a tearoom
and the chance to ride around the farm in an open wagon.

Carrickfergus Castle

Marine Highway, Carrickfergus, Co. Antrim @028/9335 1273,
@www.ehsni.gov.uk. April–May & Sept Mon–Sat 10am–6pm,
Sun 2–6pm; June–Aug Mon–Sat 10am–6pm, Sun noon–6pm;
Oct–March Mon–Sat 10am–4pm, Sun 2–4pm. Adults £3, children £1.50, family £8.
Overlooking the harbour, the castle was begun in around
1180 by the Anglo-Norman invader John de Courcy and
remained a military bastion for much of its succeeding life
(it was garrisoned until 1928). Tour guides direct you around

the castle, recounting events in its history and introducing you to the life-size models of some of its key characters – you can meet de Courcy and his wife Lady Affreca in the inner courtyard. The castle is the venue for the medieval Lughnasa Fayre on the last Saturday in July.

Flame – The Gasworks Museum of Ireland

44 Irish Quarter West, Carrickfergus, Co. Antrim ☏ 028/9336 9575, ⓦ www.gasworksflame.com. March & Oct Sat & Sun 2–6pm; April, June & Sept daily 2–6pm; July & Aug daily 10am–6pm. Adults £2.50, child £1.50 family £7.

Ireland's only surviving coal-fired gasworks was built between 1855 and 1867 to light Carrickfergus's street lamps and operated until 1964 (the Big Lamp at the end of the High Street is one of the few survivors). The gasworks has been restored by enthusiasts and now provides a diverting account of its former functions. There's also the chance to climb up to the top of the gasholder and enjoy a fine view of the town below.

T.A.C.T. Wildlife Centre

2 Crumlin Rd, Crumlin, Co. Antrim ☏ 028/9445 9739, ⓦ www.tactwildlifecentre.org.uk. Mon–Fri noon–3pm, Sun 2–5pm. Suggested donation adults £3, children £1.50.

The Talnotry Avian Care Trust looks after sick, injured and abandoned birds and small mammals, preparing them for a return to the wild whenever possible. Long-term residents on view include owls, falcons, gannets, foxes, rabbits and hedgehogs.

Giant's Causeway

Causeway Head, Co. Antrim. Open access. Giant's Causeway visitor centre ☏ 028/2073 1855, ⓦ www.northantrim.com. Daily: June 10am–6pm; July–Aug 10am–7pm; Sept–May 10am–5pm. Free, car parking £5.

The Giant's Causeway is unquestionably the most popular attraction in Northern Ireland, with crowds flocking all year round to see this bizarre formation of more than 37,000 black basalt columns, each in the shape of a polygon. So, to avoid the crowds, it's best to arrive early in the morning or late in the afternoon. The best approach to the causeway is the cliff-top path accessed from behind the visitor centre and then the steps down to the beach below. Alternatively, you can follow the road down the hill from the centre or take a minibus (£1.20 return per person).

Once there you can marvel at the unworldly scene and wonder whether the legendary giant Finn McCool really did build the causeway either to visit an inamorata or beat up another giant in Scotland. Getting to the causeway couldn't be easier. There's the narrow-gauge railway from Bushmills (☎028/2073 2844, ⊛www.giantscausewayrailway .org; March, April & Oct Sat & Sun 11am–4pm; May–Sept daily 11am–5pm; adults' return fare £5, children £3, family £14) or the regular "open topper" bus running daily in July and August from Coleraine and stopping at Portstewart, Portrush and Bushmills along the way.

Causeway School Museum

Beside Giant's Causeway Centre, Co. Antrim ☎028/2073 1777.
Daily July–Aug 11am–5pm. Adults £0.75, children £0.50, family £2.
Situated at the end of the Causeway Centre car park, the school, which functioned from 1915 to 1962, was designed by Clough Williams Ellis (famed architect of Portmeirion in Wales). The museum houses displays on the school's history while a video re-creates a day in its life during the 1920s. Children can attempt copperplate handwriting and experiment with some bygone pastimes such as spinning tops.

Carnfunnock Country Park

Drains Bay, Coast Rd, Larne, Co. Antrim ☎028/2827,
☎028/2827 0541, ⊛www.larne.gov.uk. Dawn–dusk. Car parking charge related to length of visit.
Some three miles north of Larne, Carnfunnock is a delightful country park offering plenty to suit children of all ages. As well as a maze in the shape of Northern Ireland, there's a walled garden featuring a variety of sundials, a children's activity centre (including an outdoor adventure playground), plenty of forest walks and rides on a miniature railway (Easter–Oct). The park hosts an extensive programme of events including birds of prey displays, Easter egg hunts, storytelling and a horse and pony show. There's also a nine-hole golf course and a coffee shop.

Irish Linen Centre and Lisburn Museum

Market Square, Lisburn, Co. Antrim ☎028/9266 3377,
⊛www.lisburn.gov.uk. Mon–Sat 9.30am–5pm. Free.
The museum's permanent exhibition, Flax to Fabric, recounts the history of Northern Ireland's linen industry and includes weavers plying their craft on purpose-built hand looms. The rest of the space houses temporary exhibitions and the building's modern annexe is home to the local tourist office.

Glenariff Forest Park

Glenariff, Co. Antrim ☎028/2955 6000,
⊛www.forestserviceni.gov.uk. Daily 9am–dusk. Car £4, adult pedestrian £1.50, child pedestrian £0.50.

Up in the hills above the village of Waterfoot lies this splendid forest park, renowned for its marvellous walks around the glen to mountain viewpoints. The best of these is the waymarked Waterfall Trail which takes you to a stunning series of cascades, whose beauty can be admired from the safety of a timber walkway. There's a campsite and space for touring caravans.

Ford Farm Park and Museum

8 Low Rd, Islandmagee, Co. Antrim ⓣ028/9335 3264, ⓦwww.ford-farm.co.uk. Daily March–Oct 2–6pm. Adults £2.75, children £2.50.

This working farm by the shores of Larne Lough features all manner of animals and offers demonstrations of butter-making and spinning. There's also a small museum which conveys an impression of what life must have been like for farming communities in the past.

Barry's Amusements

16 Eglinton St, Portrush, Co. Antrim ⓣ028/7082 2340, ⓦwww.barrysamusements.com. Easter–June Sat 1–10.30pm, Sun 11–10.30pm; July–Aug daily 1–10.30pm.

There's lots of indoor and outdoor fun to be had in this amusement park with rides including dodgems, cyclone, carousel, ghost train and the stomach-churning looping star (a roller coaster with an upside-down twist) plus plenty of indoor video games. The park operates a system whereby tokens (50p each) are purchased in advance, each attraction costing between one and four tokens.

Dunluce Castle

3 miles east of Portrush, Co. Antrim ⓣ028/2073 1938, ⓦwww.ehsni.gov.uk. April–May & Sept Mon–Sat 10am–6pm, Sun 2–6pm; June–Aug Mon–Sat 10am–6pm, Sun noon–6pm; Oct–March Mon–Sat 10am–4pm, Sun 2–4pm. Adults £2, children £1.

High on a headland, the ruins of sixteenth-century Dunluce Castle could not have a more dramatic setting. The McDonnells ruled from here and the castle's position was always precarious in both the political and physical sense. In 1584 it was the subject of a siege by the English and in 1639 the castle kitchen fell off the cliff during a storm. Unsurprisingly, the McDonnells left not long afterwards and the castle was abandoned, gradually falling into ruin. A tour of the remainder is well worth undertaking, as is the scramble down the cliff to a cave which goes right under the headland and has an opening directly under the castle's gatehouse.

Dunluce Centre

10 Sandhill Drive, Portrush, Co. Antrim ℡ 028/7082 4444, Ⓦ www
.touristnetuk.com/ni.dunluce. Easter week daily 10.30am–7pm;
April–May Sat & Sun noon–7pm; June, Mon–Fri 10am–5pm, Sat &
Sun noon–7pm; July–Aug daily 10.30am–7pm; Sept–March Sat &
Sun noon–5pm. £3.25 per attraction, £8 combined ticket.

The centre houses three attractions resolutely aimed at children. Finn McCool's Adventure Playground includes touch-screen games, an obstacle course, a climbing wall and the delights of a 3D twister. Treasure Fortress is a hi-tech treasure hunt where groups of two or more explore themed castle rooms, solving a quiz trail in order to release a spellbound princess and her fabulous dowry of Spanish treasure. Lastly, Turbo Tours features moving seats synchronized to respond to events in action-packed Hollywood films.

Portrush Countryside Centre and National Nature Reserve

8 Bath Rd, Portrush, Co. Antrim ℡ 028/7082 3600. June–Sept
Mon–Fri daily 10am–6pm, Sat & Sun noon–8pm. Free.

While the centre holds an exhibition on the local seashore and marine life, alongside a touch tank and live sea creatures, the adjacent nature reserve offers activities such as fossil hunts, rock pool rambles and birdwatching.

The Portrush Puffer

Portrush, Co. Antrim ℡ 028/7032 5400. July–Aug every 30min
Mon–Sat 11am–1.30pm & 2–7pm, Sun 2–7pm. Adults £1.80,
children £0.90, family day ticket £5.

This passenger road train plies its way around the town in high season and forms a handy way to enjoy the sites and visit the various attractions.

Rathlin Island

Co. Antrim.

Northern Island's only inhabited offshore island lies five miles off the coast and is easily accessible by ferry from Ballycastle (2–4 daily). Once there you can hire a bike from *Soerneog View Hostel* (℡028/2076 3954) to tour the island and discover its prehistoric remains or take the regular minibus that runs in summer between Church Bay (the ferry terminal) and Bull Point where the viewpoint at the west lighthouse (April–Aug; contact RSPB warden in advance ℡028/2076 3948) reveals the spectacle of Northern Ireland's largest colony of sea birds, including puffins and guillemots. There's a visitor centre by the harbour (May–Aug daily 10am–4pm; ℡028/2076 3951) and meals are available at *The Manor House B&B* and *McCuaig's* bar.

Patterson's Spade Mill

Templepatrick, Co. Antrim ⓣ028/9443 3619, ⓦwww.ntni.org.uk.
2–6pm: March 7–28 Sun; April 3–4 Sat & Sun; April 9–18 daily;
April 24–May 30 Sat & Sun; June 2–Aug 30 Mon & Wed–Sun;
Sept 4–Oct 10 Sat & Sun. Adult £3.60, children £2.10, family
£8.80. National Trust.

Now here's a strange one. You've almost certainly heard of
water-driven corn and flax mills, but this place is the last of
its kind in Ireland, a mill that manufactures the spades. The
spade-maker takes visitors on a tour of the premises and its
still functional hammers, turbine and press and, at the end,
will measure you should you wish to buy your own bespoke
handcrafted spade.

Derry

Tower Museum

Union Hall Place, Derry city, Co. Derry ⓣ028/7137 2411.
July–Aug Mon–Sat 10am–5pm, Sun 2–5pm; Sept–June
Tues–Sat 10am–5pm. Adults £3.65, children £2.

Housed in a re-creation of a medieval tower, this excellent
museum provides a detailed and entertaining account of the
city's history employing all manner of tableaux and audiovisual displays to enrich understanding of key elements in
Derry's development, from early beginnings to the 1688–89
siege and right up to the Troubles and the present day. At the
time of writing, funding had been obtained for a new
gallery focusing on the treasures of the Spanish Armada.

Derry city walls and city centre

The seventeenth-century walls encircling Derry's old city
are amongst the best-preserved defences in Europe and a
stroll along their mile-long walkway forms an essential part
of a visit to the city. The complete circuit takes in all manner
of bulwarks and bastions and four gateways (Shipquay,
Ferryquay, Bishop and Butcher – the gates that were shut
during the famous siege of 1688–89). It passes some of the
key sites in the city's history, such as St Columb's Cathedral,
and overlooks both the Fountain area (a small Protestant
enclave) and the Bogside, a large Nationalist area with its
political murals, Bloody Sunday memorial and Free Derry
wall.

Harbour Museum

Harbour Square, Derry city, Co. Derry ⓣ028/7137 7331.
Mon–Fri 10am–1pm & 2–4.30pm. Free.

For anyone with an interest in maritime history, the museum is well worth a visit. Its most striking exhibits are a replica of the type of boat in which St Columba is believed to have sailed to Iona in 563 AD and a real longboat found in the River Bann and dating from the fifteenth century. The museum also hosts temporary exhibitions.

Sports and activities

Adventure and activity centre

Ardclinis Outdoor Adventure High St, Cushendall, Co. Antrim ℡ 028/2177 1340, ⓦ www.ardclinis.com. Also does bike rental.

Bicycle rental

Happy Days 245 Lone Moor Rd, Derry city, Co. Derry ℡ 028/7128 7128; **Ramble Rentals** 28–30 Glenlough, Ballymoney, Co. Antrim ℡ 028/2766 6676.

Boat trips

Ballycastle Charters New Pier, Ballycastle, Co. Antrim ℡ 028/2076 2074. Runs sea-fishing trips during the summer months (Mon, Wed & Fri 7–9pm; adults £10, children £5) and provides free fishing lessons (rod, line and sinker hire £3).

Cinemas

Co. Antrim: Lisburn Omniplex Governors Rd, Lisburn ℡ 028/9266 3664; **Portrush Playhouse** Main St, Portrush ℡ 028/7082 3917.

Co. Derry: Jet Centre Dunhill Rd, Coleraine ℡ 028/7032 9909; **Orchard Hall** Orchard St, Derry ℡ 028/7126 2845; **Regal** Main St, Limavady ℡ 028/7776 6158; **Strand** Strand Rd, Derry ℡ 028/7137 3000.

Go-karting

Raceview Indoor Karting 1 Woodside Rd, Woodside Industrial Estate, Ballymena, Co. Antrim ℡ 028/2565 1000, ⓦ www .raceviewindoorkarting.co.uk.

Horse riding

Co. Antrim: Castle Hill Equestrian Centre 86 Fenagh Rd, Ballymena ℡ 028/2588 1222; **Hillmount Equestrian Centre** 6 Straid Rd, Ballycastle ℡ 028/2076 2686; **Islandmagee Riding Centre** 103 Brown's Bay Rd, Islandmagee ℡ 028/9338 2108,

@ www.islandmagee.co.uk; **Maddybenny Riding Centre** 11
Maddybenny Park, Portrush ⓣ 028/7082 3394, @ www
.maddybenny.freeserve.co.uk; **The Rainbow Equestrian Centre**
24 Hollow Rd, Islandmagee ⓣ 028/9338 2929, @ www
.activityholsni.co.uk.

Co. Derry: **Ardmore Stables** 8 Rushall Rd, Ardmore
ⓣ 028/7134 5187; **Banagher Equestrian Centre** 86 Glenedra
Rd, Feeny ⓣ 028/7778 1117; **Cool Riding Stables** 68A
Ballynahedin Rd, Claudy ⓣ 028/7133 8277; **Faughanvale Pony
Trekking Centre** 11 Dunedra Rd, Greysteel ⓣ 028/7181 1843;
Hill Farm Equestrian Centre 47 Aitikeeragh Rd, Castlerock
ⓣ 028/7084 8629; **The Island Equestrian Centre** 49
Ballyrashane Rd, Coleraine ⓣ 028/7034 2599; **Streeve Hill
House** 25 Dowland Rd, Limavady ⓣ 028/7776 6563; **Timbertop**
Riding Centre, 60 Curran Rd, Aghadowey ⓣ 028/7086 8788.

Pitch and putt

Ballyreagh Putting Green Portrush, Co. Antrim ⓣ 028/7082
2028; **Curran Park** Larne, Co. Antrim ⓣ 028/2826 0088; **Royal
Portrush Golf Club** Portrush, Co. Antrim ⓣ 028/7082 2311;
Town Park Larne, Co. Antrim ⓣ 028/2826 0478.

Surfing

The main surfing beaches are at Castlerock and Portstewart,
Co. Derry, and Portballintrae and Portush, Co. Antrim (West
Strand, East Strand and White Rocks). A daily surf report is
available on ⓣ 0839/337 770 and boards can be rented at several outlets in Portrush and Portstewart. Summer surfing is generally fine, with waves rising to no more than 6ft, but can be very
dangerous at other times.

Swimming

Lagan Valley Leisureplex Lisburn Leisure Park, Lisburn, Co.
Antrim ⓣ028/9267 2121, @ www.lisburn.gov.uk. Leisure pool:
Mon–Fri 3.30–5.30pm & 6.30–8.30pm (Thurs & Fri until 9pm), Sat
& Sun 10am–5.30pm; adults £4.60, children £3.20 (under 5s free),
family £12.80. The North's premier swimming complex, offering
competition and diving pools as well as a leisure pool featuring a
huge galleon, master-blaster water cannons and tyre rides. Note
that the centre is open longer hours during school holidays and
that there's a special Lazy River family session each Saturday
morning, 10–11am; adults £2.20, children £1.50, under 5s free.

Waterworld The Harbour, Portrush, Co. Antrim ⓣ 028/7082
2001. Easter week & July–Aug Mon–Sat 10am–8pm, Sun
noon–8pm; May & Sept Sat 10am–7pm, Sun noon–7pm; June
Mon–Sat 10am–7pm, Sun noon–7pm; £4.50. A fun swimming
pool with flumes, slides and power-blasting cannons.

Ten-pin bowling

Brunswick Superbowl Wakehurst Rd, Ballymena, Co. Antrim
☎028/2564 4144, ⓦwww.sportsbowl.com. This has ball walls
available to help children score every time and also features an
indoor adventure castle, containing a variety of swings and
obstacles, plus plenty of video games and a restaurant.

Accommodation

Benone Tourist Complex 53 Benone Ave, Benone, Magilligan,
Co. Derry ☎028/7755 0555. *Benone* is set by a wonderful Blue
Flag beach and has heated splash pools, tennis courts, and an
adventure play area. Perfect if you're camping or have a touring
caravan or RV.

City Hotel Queen's Quay, Derry city, Co. Derry ☎028/7136
5800, ⓦwww.greatsouthernhotels.com. Absolutely plush new
city-centre hotel, offering views of the River Foyle, and its own
swimming pool and gym.

Maddybenny Farmhouse 18 Maddybenny Park, Portrush, Co.
Antrim ☎028/7082 3394, ⓦwww.maddybenny.freeserve.co.uk.
Rural farmhouse with superb rooms with great breakfasts (child
reductions); also has its own riding centre, a games room and
self-catering cottages.

The Manor House Rathlin Island, Co. Antrim ☎028/2076 2964,
ⓦwww.ntni.org.uk. Large, well-equipped guesthouse owned by
the National Trust and set right by the waterside.

Marine Hotel 1 North St, Ballycastle, Co. Antrim ☎028/2076
2222, ⓦwww.marinehotel.net. With sea views and its own
indoor swimming pool, the *Marine* makes a comfortable place to
stay; substantial child reductions.

The Saddler's House 36 Great James St, Derry city, Co. Derry
☎028/7126 9691, ⓦwww.thesaddlershouse.com. Superb city-
centre B&B both here and at the same owners' nearby
Merchant's House at 16 Queen St (same contact details). Also
on offer is a self-catering cottage bang in the centre of the old
city.

Places to eat

Bushmills Inn Hotel 9 Dunluce Rd, Bushmills, Co. Antrim
☎028/2073 2339. Old coaching inn with turf fires and gas light-
ing, serving splendid bar and restaurant meals and a hugely
popular Sunday carvery lunch.

Harry's 10 Mill St, Cushendall, Co. Antrim ⓣ028/2177 2022. Huge portions and a very extensive menu, including regular daily specials, at this family-friendly bar-restaurant.

Londonderry Arms Hotel 20–28 Harbour Rd, Carnlough, Co. Antrim ⓣ028/2888 5255. Owned briefly during the 1920s by Winston Churchill, this hotel serves excellent lunches and dinners, including its speciality, Glenarm smoked salmon.

Morelli's 53–58 The Promenade, Portstewart, Co. Derry. Newly refurbished café serving everything from snacks to full-scale Italian meals with its own justifiably lauded ice cream.

16
Down and Armagh

The neighbouring counties of Down and Armagh occupy the southeastern corner of Northern Ireland. Down is very much a seafaring county, its coastline running east from Belfast, then down the Ards Peninsula, almost enclosing the marvellous Strangford

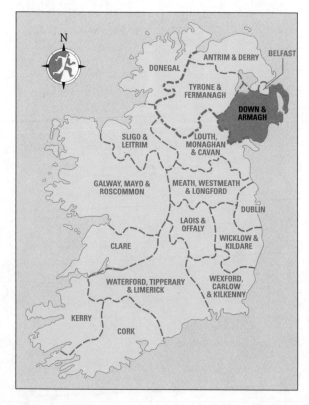

Lough, before heading west along Carlingford Lough to Newry. Not surprisingly, the county has several popular seaside resorts, the best known being Bangor, Newcastle and Warrenpoint. Between Newcastle and Rostrevor lie the beguiling peaks of the Mourne Mountains and, if you'd like to walk amongst them, it's well worth visiting the Mourne Heritage Trust, 87 Central Promenade (☎028/4372 4059; Mon–Fri 9am–5pm) which can advise on the best routes for children.

Alternatively, the Mourne Rambler bus takes a circular route through the mountains, starting at Newcastle (☎028/4372 2296; July & Aug Mon–Sat 10.10am, 11.35am, 2.05pm, 3.30pm; adults £4, children £2). County Armagh is completely landlocked, but still has plenty of interesting countryside and attractions, the latter not least in the ecclesiastical city of Armagh itself. There's also plenty to see and do around the southern shores of Lough Neagh and in the rural lands surrounding Slieve Gullion in South Armagh.

County Down

Pickie Family Fun Park

The Promenade, Bangor, Co. Down ☎028/9127 4430. March 17 to Oct, daily 9am–dusk; Nov–March 16, Sat & Sun 9am–dusk. Prices per ride.

Situated on the western side of Bangor's Marina, the fun park's attractions include pedal boats disguised as swans, a miniature railway, go-karts, a superslide, paddling pools and an adventure playground. Prices range from £1.25 for a train ride to £3 for a pedal boat (seats three).

BANGOR

Castle Espie Wildfowl and Wetlands Centre

Ballydrain Rd, Comber, Co. Down ⓣ 028/9187 4146, ⓦ www.wwt.org.uk. March–June & Sept–Oct Mon–Fri 10.30am–5pm, Sat & Sun 11am–5pm; July & Aug Mon–Fri 10.30am–5.30pm, Sat & Sun 11am–5.30pm; Nov–Feb Mon–Fri 11am–4pm, Sat & Sun 11am–4.30pm. Adults £4.60, children £2.75 (under 4s free), family £11.95.

Signposted south of Comber on the A22, Castle Espie is home to both native wildfowl and endangered species from other countries which can be viewed from hides, in water-fowl gardens and along woodland walks, allowing children to get "nose to beak" to some of the rarest swans, ducks and geese in the world. In spring and summer there are hundreds of ducklings and flocks of waders and Brent geese arrive in winter. The centre also has an excellent book shop offering further information, a coffee shop and a children's play area.

Ulster Folk and Transport Museum

Cultra, Co. Down ⓣ 028/9042 8428, ⓦ www.magni.org. March–Sept, Mon–Fri 10am–5pm (July–Sept until 6pm), Sat 10am–6pm, Sun 11am–6pm; Oct–Feb closes one hour earlier each day. Folk museum or transport museum: adults £4.50, children £2.50, family £12; combined ticket: adults £6, children £3, family £13.

You'll need at least a day to explore these two museums, occupying a huge site straddling the main A2 Belfast-Bangor road. The Folk Museum is focused on the mythical town of Ballycultra in the early 1900s, whose real buildings have been taken from various parts of Northern Ireland, and is populated by costumed guides. The town also has its own adjacent countryside with farms, cottages and livestock. The Transport Museum has a superb collection of rail and road transport and re-created Belfast street scenes while its "Flight Experience" exhibition examines aviation history through films, aircraft models and engineering interactives. Finally, the *Titanic* exhibition focuses on the construction in Belfast of the doomed ship, supplying plenty of photographs and contemporary newsreels.

Down County Museum

English St, Downpatrick, Co. Down ⓣ 028/4461 5218, ⓦ www.downcountymuseum.com. Mon–Fri 10am–5pm, Sat & Sun 1–5pm. Free.

The town's former gaol and Governor's house, built in the eighteenth century, contain some reasonably interesting displays on local history and rather more interesting temporary exhibitions. However, the cell block is certainly worth a visit, each cell having been restored to period conditions and several containing tableaux, such as a group of five men charged with causing an affray at Strangford Pier in 1814 and two women found guilty of passing forged banknotes. Look out for the giant chess and draughts sets in the courtyard.

Downpatrick Railway Museum

Railway Station, Market St, Downpatrick, Co. Down ⊤028/4461 5779, ⓦwww.downpatricksteamrailway.co.uk. Sat 10am–4pm, also June–Aug Mon–Fri 11am–2pm. Prices dependent on type of train trip; child discounts and family tickets available.

The town's old station houses a model railway and displays related to the former Belfast and County Down Railway which ran from Belfast to Newcastle. There are steam train trips on Saturday afternoons in July and August and on some public holidays, plus a special Hallowe'en service and Christmas specials.

Quoile Countryside Centre

5 Quay Rd, Downpatrick, Co. Down ⊤028/4461 3280, ⓦwww.ehsni.gov.uk. April–Aug daily 11am–5pm; Sept–March Sat & Sun 1–5pm. Free.

Despite its address, this centre is actually a couple of miles north of Downpatrick, off the A25. Its displays describe the wildlife of the Quoile Pondage which was created when a barrage was built to prevent local flooding, changing the saltwater estuary to a freshwater habitat. Outside there are various woodlands and wetlands to explore and wildfowl to be spotted, along with their nest hidden in reeds on the riverbank. The centre organizes nature rambles and seal-watching sessions on Strangford Lough.

Murlough National Nature Reserve

Dundrum, Co. Down ⊤028/4375 1467, ⓦwww.ntni.org.uk. Open access all year. May to mid-Sept car £2.

Murlough offers a splendid way to enjoy the delights of Dundrum Bay and also provides an alternative (and far more interesting) access to Newcastle beach. There's a self-guided nature trail here which follows a series of paths and boardwalks, taking in a variety of butterfly and bird life, as well as plenty of wild flowers and magnificent views of the Mournes.

Silent Valley

4 miles north of Kilkeel, Co. Down ⊤028/9074 1166. April–Sept 10am–6.30pm; Oct–March 10am–4pm. Car £3, adult pedestrian £1.50, child pedestrian £0.50.

The Silent Valley and Ben Crom reservoirs supply much of Belfast and Co. Down's water and a view of the dams themselves makes a terrific sight. The three-mile circular Viewpoint Walk takes in spectacular scenes of the Mourne Mountains while the half-mile Sally Lough stroll takes you up to the dam at Ben Crom (alternatively, there's a shuttle bus May, June & Sept noon–5.45pm, July–Aug noon–6pm; return trip: adults £1.50, children £0.90).

Ballycopeland Windmill

1 mile west of Millisle, Co. Down ⓣ 028/9054 3037, ⓦ www.ehsni.gov.uk. July–Aug Tues & Fri–Sun 2–6pm, Wed & Thurs 10am–1pm.

This tower mill dates from the late eighteenth century and was in operation until 1915. Restored and maintained, the mill is the only one still functioning in the county and offers visitors the chance to see how it works and to try their hand at milling. The former miller's cottage also has a working model of the mill.

Coco's Indoor Adventure Playground

27A Central Promenade, Newcastle, Co. Down. ⓣ 028/4372 6226, ⓦ www.cocosplayground.com. June–Aug daily 10am–9pm; Sept–May Mon–Thurs 1.30–8pm, Sat & Sun 10am–8pm. Children £4, toddlers £3.

This indoor soft play area offers a handy alternative on rainy days. There's a variety of slides (including snake, astra and tube), an assault course, a bouncy castle and ball pools while toddlers have their own supervised play area.

Ark Open Farm

296 Bangor Rd, Newtownards, Co. Down ⓣ 028/9182 0445, ⓦ www.thearkopenfarm.co.uk. Mon–Sat 10am–6pm, Sun 2–6pm. Adults £2.90, children £2.10.

The Ark was Ireland's first public rare breeds farm and features animals such as the Irish Moiled and Kerry cattle, as well as llamas, a variety of ducks and poultry, sheep, goats and pigs (including the Vietnamese pot-bellied breed). There are also both indoor and outdoor children's play areas and a tearoom.

Exploris Aquarium

The Rope Walk, Castle St, Portaferry, Co. Down ⓣ 028/4272 8062, ⓦ www.exploris.org.uk. April–Aug Mon–Fri 10am–6pm, Sat 11am–6pm, Sun noon–6pm; Sept–March closes one hour earlier. Adults £6.20, children £3.70, family £17.50.

One of the county's most popular attractions, Exploris

provides a real and entertaining insight into the lives of marine creatures. Touch tanks allow visitors to feel and hold creatures as varied as rays and spiny starfish, while an open sea tank (containing a quarter of a million litres of water) reveals a massive range of sea life, including sharks. Elsewhere there's the marine discovery laboratory (where microscopic embryos can be observed) and a jellyfish display. Seals are a regular feature of Strangford Lough and Exploris has recently opened a sanctuary for sick and orphaned seal pups, preparing them for a return to the Lough.

Tropical Butterfly House and Gardens

Seaforde Demesne, Seaforde, Co. Down ⓣ 028/4481 1225, ⓦ www.seafordegardens.com. Easter–Sept Mon–Sat 10am–5pm, Sun 1–6pm. Butterfly house: adults £3, children £2; combined butterfly house and gardens ticket: adults £5.50, children £3.

A trip to the Butterfly House is an absolute must for the chance to see hundreds of giant, brightly coloured free-flying butterflies, as well a variety of somewhat ferocious-looking tropical insects and reptiles kept, fortunately, in glass cases. The blissful walled garden includes many rare and beautiful plants, as well as a maze which leads to a pavilion covered in roses.

Castle Ward

Strangford, Co. Down ⓣ 028/4488 1204, ⓦ www.ntni.org.uk. Grounds: daily 10am–8pm (Oct–April close at 4pm). Adults £3.10, children £1.30, family £7.30; house and wildlife centre: May Wed–Sun noon–6pm; June–Aug daily noon–6pm (June Mon–Fri opens 1pm); Sept–Oct Sat & Sun noon–6pm; combined house, wildlife centre and grounds ticket: adults £4.70, children £1.80, family £9.90. National Trust.

A little way down the Downpatrick road from Strangford lies Castle Ward, an opulent eighteenth-century mansion set in gorgeous grounds. In June the estate stages an annual opera festival (ⓣ 028/9066 1090 for details), but for the rest of the summer season, it's the house which draws fascinated crowds. For children, however, the real attractions are the wildlife centre (which depicts and interprets marine and bird life found around Strangford Lough), the restored corn mill, the many trails and the Victorian playroom. The grounds are a great place for a picnic (there are tables by the lough) and you can camp here too (ⓣ 028/4488 1680).

SEAFORDE • STRANGFORD

Armagh

Armagh Planetarium

College Hill, Armagh city, Co. Armagh ⊤028/3752 4725,
Ⓦwww.armaghplanet.com. Mon–Fri 1.45–4.45pm. Adults £3,
children £2, family £9.

The planetarium is still undergoing refurbishment and the
main reason for visiting is the daily audiovisual show which
takes place at 3pm, whose digital projectors take the audience on an absorbing journey through the universe; advance
booking recommended.

Palace Stables Heritage Centre

Friary Rd, Armagh city, Co. Armagh ⊤028/3752 9629,
Ⓦwww.visitarmagh.com. Mon–Sat 10am–5pm, Sun 2–5pm.

Next to the Archbishop's Palace, the former home of the
Primates of the Church of Ireland, stands this restored
Georgian stable block. Inside there's a permanent theatrical
display, "A Day in the Life", in which costumed interpreters
re-create the day in 1776 when Archbishop Robinson
entertained the English agriculturalist and writer Arthur
Young, featuring the archbishop himself, guests and servants.
You can also see the servants' tunnel which connected the
kitchens to the house (Robinson loathed the smell of cooking) while outside there's a well-preserved ice house, a sensory garden (featuring wind chimes and fountains) and, by
the car park, an adventure playground.

St Patrick's Trian Visitor Complex

English St, Armagh city, Co. Armagh ⊤028/3752 1801,
Ⓦwww.visitarmagh.com. Mon–Sat 10am–5pm, Sun 2–5pm.
Adults £4, children £2.25, family £10.

Apart from containing the tourist office, this complex also
houses three multimedia entertainments aimed at children of
different ages. In "The Land of Lilliput" a twenty-foot giant
tells the story of *Gulliver's Travels* (whose author, Jonathan
Swift, had connections with Armagh). "The Armagh Story"
provides a colourful account of the city's history while
"Patrick's Testament" is an interactive explanation of the
saint's association with the city.

Lough Neagh Discovery Centre

Oxford Island National Nature Reserve, Craigavon, Co. Armagh
⊤028/3832 2205, Ⓦwww.oxfordisland.com. April–Sept
Mon–Sat 10am–6pm, Sun 10am–7pm; Oct–March Wed–Sun
10am–5pm. Adults £4, children £2.

The centre's focus is on the history, culture and ecology of

Lough Neagh, but it treats its subject in a very lively way, through interactive games and audiovisual shows. There are several miles of trails around the lough as well as bird-watching hides, while the centre also provides guided walks and runs an extensive programme of events throughout the year.

The Argory

Derrycaw Rd, Moy, Co. Armagh ⓣ 028/8778 4753, ⓦ www.ntni.org.uk. Grounds: daily 10am–8pm (Oct–April close 4pm); house: mid-March to May & Sept, Sat & Sun noon–6pm; June Mon–Fri 1–6pm, Sat & Sun noon–6pm; July–Aug daily noon–6pm. Grounds and house tour: adults £4.10, children £2.10, family £10.40. Car £2.10;

Four miles east of Moy, this superb Neoclassical mansion dates from 1824 and sits amidst gorgeous gardens and an expansive wooded estate by the River Blackwater. Still lit by an original 1906 acetylene gas plant, the house's rooms contain an astonishing panoply of original Victorian and Edwardian furniture and period items, including a sumptuous cabinet barrel organ (which actually gets played during special musical house tours – call for details). Various events, such as a Victorian Sunday, are also mounted here each month.

Ardress House

64 Ardress Rd, Portadown, Co. Armagh ⓣ 028/3885 1236, ⓦ www.ntni.org.uk. Mid-March to May & Sept, Sat & Sun; June & Aug Wed–Mon 2–6pm. Adults £2.80, children £1.40, family £7. National Trust.

Set deep in apple orchard country, this seventeenth-century farmhouse, much extended in the following century, can be enjoyed in the company of costumed guides. The interior includes a splendid art collection. Children will probably be more interested in the farmyard and its traditional implements (which can be handled); and there's a playground, too, as well as pleasant gardens and riverside walks. Despite its postal address the house is actually five miles from Portadown on the B28 Moy road.

Sports and activities

Adventure and activity centres

Blue Lough Mountain and Watersport Centre The Grange Courtyard, Castlewellan Forest Park, Main St, Castlewellan, Co.

Down ⊤028/4377 0715; **Tollymore Mountain Centre**
Bryansford, Newcastle, Co. Down ⊤028/4372 2158, ⓦwww
.tollymoremc.com; **Waterside House Activity Centre** Kinnego
Bay, Craigavon, Co. Armagh ⊤028/3832 7573.

Boat cruises

Bangor Harbour Boats Bangor Marina, Co. Down ⊤028/9145
5321, ⓦwww.kingdomsofdown.com/bangorharbourboats.
Offers pleasure cruises around Belfast Lough and fishing trips
from Easter to October.

Kinnego Marina Boat trips on Lough Neagh, Co. Armagh.
April–Oct, Sat & Sun, every 30min 1.30–6.30pm; adults £4, children £2.

Nelson's Boats 14B Killaughy Rd, Donaghadee, Co. Down
⊤028/9188 3403, ⓦwww.kingdomsofdown.com/nelsonsboats.
Runs visits to the deserted Copeland Islands and offers fishing
trips from June to September.

Strangford Charter 6 Sketrick Island, Killinchy, Co. Down
⊤028/9754 1564, ⓦwww.kingdomsofdown.com
/strangfordcharter. Operates a regular tour of Strangford Lough
(May–Sept Sat & Sun 3pm; £6 per person).

Cinemas

Co Down: Bangor Multiplex 1 Valentines Rd, Castle Park,
Bangor ⊤028/9146 5007; **Iveagh Cinema** Huntly Rd,
Banbridge ⊤028/4066 2423; **Movieland** Ards Shopping Centre,
Blair Main Rd South, Newtownards ⊤028/9182 1000,
ⓦwww.movieland.co.uk; **Newry Omniplex Cinema** Quays
Shopping Centre, Albert Basin, Newry ⊤028/3025 2237.

Co. Armagh: City Film House Market Place, Armagh city, Co.
Armagh ⊤028/3751 1033; **Centre Point Cinemas** Portadown
Rd, Lurgan ⊤028/3832 4667.

Go-karting

Gosford Karting 49 Dinnahorra Rd, Markethill, Co. Armagh
⊤028/3755 1248.

Horse riding

Co. Down: Ardminnan Equestrian Centre 15 Ardminnan Rd,
Portaferry ⊤028/4277 1321; **Drumgooland House and
Equestrian Centre** 29 Dunnanew Rd, Seaforde ⊤028/4481
1956, ⓦwww.horsetrek-ireland.com; **Gransha Equestrian
Centre** 10 Kerrs Rd, 6 Road Ends, Bangor ⊤028/9181 3313;
Mourne Trail Riding Centre 96 Castlewellan Rd, Newcastle
⊤028/4372 4351, ⓦwww.mournetrailridingcentre.com;
Oakwood Riding School 24 Benagh Rd, Newry ⊤028/3085

1485; **Tullymurray Equestrian Centre** 145 Ballydugan Rd,
Downpatrick ⓣ028/4481 1880.

Co. Armagh: Greenvale Trekking Centre 141 Longfield Rd,
Forkhill ⓣ028/3088 8314; **Millbrook Equestrian Centre** 1A
Crabtree Hill, Bessbrook ⓣ028/3083 8336; **Ring of Gullion
Trekking Centre** Lough Rd, Mullaghbawn, ⓣ028/3088 9311.

Swimming

Newcastle Centre and Tropicana 10–14 Central Promenade,
Newcastle ⓣ028/4372 5034. **Centre**: Mon–Fri 10am–10pm, Sat
10am–5.30pm, Sun 2–6pm; charge for various activities.
Tropicana: June–Aug, Sat 11am–5.30pm, Sun 1–6pm;
July–Aug, Mon, Wed–Fri 11am–6.45pm, Tues 11am–5pm &
6–8pm. Adults £2.50, children under 8 £2, family £12. Warm-
water outdoor swimming pool, plus badminton, table tennis and
a crèche for 3- to 5-year-olds (July–Aug, Mon–Fri
10.30am–12.30pm & 2–4pm; £3.50 per session) in the adjacent
Newcastle Centre. The centre also houses the tourist office and
stages a summer concert programme outside (July–Aug Sun
2–4pm; free).

Accommodation

Burford Lodge 30 Quay St, Ardglass, Co. Down ⓣ028/4484
1141, ⓦwww.kingdomsofdown.com/burfordlodge. Very comfortable B&B overlooking the harbour.

Burrendale Hotel and Country Club 51 Castlewellan Rd,
Newcastle, Co. Down ⓣ028/4372 2599,
ⓦwww.burrendale.com. This family-friendly hotel has a games
room, offers a listening service and organizes various family
events throughout the year.

De-Averell House No. 3 Seven Houses, 47 Upper English St,
Armagh city, Co. Armagh ⓣ028/3751 1213, ⓦwww
.deaverellhouse.com. Superb en-suite rooms in the centre of the
city with a family room and an innovative basement restaurant.

Denvir's 14–16 English St, Downpatrick, Co. Down ⓣ028/4461
2012, ⓦwww.kingdomsofdown.com/denvirs. An old coaching
inn with spacious rooms and a very child-friendly restaurant
serving sumptuous food.

The Narrows 8 Shore Rd, Portaferry, Co. Down ⓣ028/4272
8148, ⓦwww.narrows.co.uk. Exceptional guesthouse where
every room overlooks Strangford Lough which has a family
room and a splendid restaurant downstairs.

Places to eat

The Brass Monkey 16 Trevor Hill, Newry, Co. Down ⓣ028/3026 3176. Bar redecked in farmhouse fashion with a range of excellent bar, carvery and restaurant meals.

The Duke 7 Duke St, Warrenpoint, Co. Down ⓣ028/4175 2084. Astonishingly good bar meals (fresh fish is a speciality) with rather more pricey restaurant options.

The Famous Grouse 16 Ballyhagen Rd, Loughgall, Co. Armagh ⓣ028/3889 1778. Justly lauded pub, serving a range of substantial bar and restaurant meals.

Hearty's Folk Cottage Glassdrummond, Co. Armagh ⓣ028/3028 1916. Sun 2–6pm. Free. There's nowhere quite like *Hearty's* – a place where you can sit and enjoy traditional music over a pot of tea and a plate of scones, and there are plenty of examples of local craftwork on sale too.

Johnston's Café Scotch St, Armagh city, Co. Armagh. Good daytime café with everything from tea and scones to full lunches.

The Quayside The Quay, Ardglass, Co. Down. Fabulous freshly caught fish plus chips, served in this all-day café, plus a grand range of ice creams too.

17

Tyrone and Fermanagh

ounty Tyrone spreads all the way from Lough Neagh (Ireland's largest lake) in the east to its border with County Donegal in the west. It's a predominantly rural county whose main scenic attraction is the Sperrin Mountain range, a wild and lonely place offering splendid walks, though Omagh is an attractive small town and makes a fine base for exploring the region. County Fermanagh's greatest attraction is unquestionably Lough Erne, a complex of waterways and islands centred upon the cheerful town of Enniskillen. While the lough offers many opportunities for angling, boating and water sports, the county also has a number of superb forest parks, providing enjoyable walks and often splendid views (contact ☎028/6634 3032 or ⓦwww.forestserviceni.gov.uk for details).

Information

Co. Tyrone has tourist offices at: Cookstown ☎028/8676 6727; Killymaddy ☎028/8776 7259; Omagh ☎028/8224 7831; and Strabane ☎028/7188 3735. Websites providing information on the most visited parts of the county include ⓦwww .omagh.gov.uk and ⓦwww.strabanedc.com.

Co. Fermanagh's only tourist office is in Enniskillen ☎028/ 6632 3110, and Internet information is online at ⓦwww .fermanaghlakelands.com and ⓦwww.fermanagh-online.com.

Tyrone

Wellbrook Beetling Mill

20 Wellbrook Rd, Corkhill, Co. Tyrone ℡ 028/8674 8210,
ⓦ www.ntni.org.uk. Mid-March to June & Sept Sat & Sun
noon–6pm; July & Aug daily noon–6pm. Adults £2.60, children
£1.30, family £5.70. National Trust.

Scutch, hackle and weave in this re-creation of one of the
key components of the Irish linen industry, a working
water-driven flax mill whose costumed guides explain how
the whole process worked. As for the beetles, they're not
what you might imagine, but you'll just have to visit to learn
the answer!

An Creagán Visitor Centre

Creggan, Co. Tyrone ℡ 028/8076 1112, ⓦ www
.an-creagan.com. April–Sept daily 11am–6.30pm; Oct–March
Mon–Fri 11am–4.30pm. Adults £2, children £1, family £5.

Just off the A505 Cookstown-Omagh road, the centre has been designed to reflect the archaeological sites of the area. Its interpretative exhibition explores the area's environmental and archaeological heritage while informing much about its traditions and culture. The centre also provides details of local walks and places to hire cycles. It houses a fine restaurant and stages a programme of traditional music, dancing and storytelling events.

Beaghmore Stone Circles

3 miles north of Dunnamore, Co. Tyrone. Open access.

The stone circles are well signposted around four miles east of Creggan on the A505 Omagh-Cookstown road and they're well worth a detour to this isolated spot if you are in the area. Tyrone has many archaeological remains, indeed there are more than one thousand standing stones in the Sperrin Mountains alone, but the Beaghmore circles take some beating. None of the stones is more than 3ft high; there are seven circles, ten rows and a dozen burial mounds surmounted by cairns. The circles are paired except one, known as Dragon's Teeth, which has over eight hundred stones.

Aladdin's Kingdom

Mountjoy Rd, Omagh, Co. Tyrone ☎ 028/8225 1550. Mon–Thurs & Sun 2–7pm, Fri 2–9pm, Sat 10.30am–7pm (opens at 11.30am daily on school holiday weekdays). Children Mon–Fri £2, Sat £2.50.

An exciting indoor adventure playground, Aladdin's Kingdom offers a variety of slides, tunnels, rope bridges, climbing frames, a haunted house and a giant ball pool.

Ulster-American Folk Park

Castletown, Omagh, Co. Tyrone ☎ 028/8224 3292, ⓦ www .folkpark.com. Easter–Sept Mon–Sat 11am–6pm, Sun 11am–7pm; Oct–Easter Mon–Fri 10.30am–5pm. Adults £4.50, children £2.50, family £11.

One of the most enjoyable attractions in Northern Ireland, this doesn't just recount the history of emigration from Ireland to the USA but re-enacts it. The story of the emigrants is told in the indoor gallery, but it's outside where the real fun lies. Here you'll find original period buildings which have been moved from other parts of the country or recently constructed replicas and a host of costumed guides populating them and the surrounding "streets". There are thatched buildings, log cabins, a spirit grocery, chapel and meeting house and, best of all, a full-size replica brig, demonstrating the arduous conditions emigrants faced while crossing the Atlantic.

Gortin Glen Forest Park

Gortin, Co. Tyrone ⓣ028/8167 0666,
ⓦwww.forestserviceni.gov.uk. Daily 10am–dusk. Car £2.50,
adult pedestrian £1, child pedestrian £0.50.

Set on the western edge of the Sperrin Mountains, Gortin
Glen is one of the North's best forest parks, with a host of
possibilities for walkers and mountain bikers or anyone just
wanting to enjoy the countryside. There's a five-mile forest
drive which offers some breathtaking views of the mountains and three very different waymarked walking trails
(none more than a couple of miles in length). You'll also find
three mountain-bike trails and a campsite and a herd of Sika
deer.

Barrontop Fun Farm

35 Barron Rd, Donemana, Strabane, Co. Tyrone ⓣ028/7139
8649, ⓦwww.barrontop.com. March 17–June Mon–Fri
9.30am–2pm, Sat 9.30am–5pm, Sun 2pm–5pm; July & Aug &
Easter Mon–Sat 9.30am–5pm, Sun 2–5pm; Nov 23–Dec 23:
Mon–Thurs 10am–2.30pm, Fri & Sat 10am–8pm, Sun 2–6pm. £3
per person.

This farm offers the chance to see, feed and handle many
types of farm animals, and also to say hello to a kangaroo,
ostriches, emus and potbellied pigs. There's also an adventure
playground, bouncy castle and special pre-Christmas events
with Santa and a Nativity show.

Sperrin Heritage Centre

274 Glenelly Rd, Cranagh, Gortin, Co. Tyrone ⓣ028/8164 8142,
ⓦwww.strabanedc.com. April–Oct Mon–Fri 11.30am–5.30pm,
Sat 11.30–6pm, Sun 2–6pm. Adults £2.30, children £1.40, family
£7.10.

Cranagh is one of the North's most isolated communities,
set deep in the Sperrin Mountains by the Glenelly Valley.
The Heritage Centre provides a multimedia account of life
in the area, from local customs to the quest for the gold
present in the region's rich geological structure. Should you
be tempted to join the hunt, the centre will rent you a gold
pan (adults £0.65, children £0.35) and direct you towards
local streams, but don't give up the day job! There's also a
very good café here serving excellent home-made food. The
centre hosts regular Sunday afternoon traditional music
sessions.

Ulster History Park

Cullion, Gortin, Co. Tyrone ⓣ028/8164 8188,
ⓦwww.omagh.gov.uk/historypark.htm. March, Oct & Nov
Mon–Fri 10am–5pm; April–June & Sept daily 10.30am–5.30pm;

July & Aug daily 10am–6.30pm. Adults £3.75, children £2.50, family £12.

Not so much a history of the Irish people as a history of where they lived, the park features a range of full-scale reconstructions of buildings dating right back to the Stone Age and including a medieval castle and seventeenth-century Plantation residence. Inside there are videos and displays which provide further information about the dwellings and their various inhabitants. A special Family Fun Day takes place in August.

Fermanagh

ExplorErne

Erne Gateway Centre, Belleek, Co. Fermanagh ⓣ 028 6865 8866, ⓦ www.fermanagh.gov.uk. June–Sept Wed–Sun 11am–5pm. Adults £1, children 50p, family £2.

If you're heading towards Lough Erne and its environs, then this exhibition provides an informative introduction to the area. Various displays and a video tell the story of the lough's formation and its influence on local life and customs. There's also information on local monuments and castles, landscapes and wildlife.

Brookeborough Vintage Cycle Museum

Main St, Brookeborough, Co. Fermanagh ⓣ 028/8953 1206. Easter–Sept Mon–Fri 5–8pm, Sat & bank holidays 2pm–8pm. Adults £2, children £1, family £5.

This ever-expanding collection now holds more than one hundred bicycles and tricycles, including tandems, a butcher's bike and a real old gem from the 1870s powered by levers rather than pedals. There's also a wealth of old toys to see, and the museum's owner has a collection of novelty teapots.

Enniskillen Castle and Museums

Castle Barracks, Enniskillen, Co. Fermanagh ⓣ 028/6632 5000, ⓦ www.enniskillencastle.co.uk. May–Sept Mon & Sat 2–5pm, Tues–Fri 10am–5pm; July & Aug also Sun 2–5pm; Oct–April Mon 2–5pm, Tues–Fri 10am–5pm. Adults £2.50, children £1, under 5s free.

Enniskillen Castle has played four roles during its six-hundred-year existence. It began its life as a fort of the local Maguire chieftains, then was captured by the English in the early seventeenth century and rebuilt and extended, subsequently becoming a barracks and now containing two museums. The Fermanagh County Museum focuses on local history and wildlife while the Regimental Museum of the Royal Inniskillin Fusiliers celebrates the regiment through a display of its uniforms, flags and military paraphernalia.

Cole's Monument

Forthill Park, Enniskillen, Co. Fermanagh ⊤028/6632 5050. Late May to early Sept daily 1–6pm. Adults £0.70, children £0.30.
Tickets are purchased at the tourist office, not at the monument. Built between 1845 and 1857 to honour one of Wellington's generals, Sir Galbraith Lowry-Cole, this monument's 108 steps lead to a viewing platform providing panoramic views of the town and surrounding countryside. Children must be accompanied by adults.

Devenish Island

Lower Lough Erne, Co. Fermanagh, ferry ⊤07702 052873.
Easter–Sept daily at 10am, 1pm, 3pm & 5pm. Adults £2.25, children £1.20.
Devenish is the easiest of Lough Erne's numerous islands to visit and in many ways the most rewarding. The ferry operates from Trory Point, signposted just before the Kesh turn-off on the A32 Enniskillen-Irvinestown road. Once on the island you'll discover the remains of a monastic community, founded in the sixth century, including an oratory, round tower, a thirteenth-century church and a ruined priory, as well as one of Ireland's most superb high crosses.

Marble Arch Caves and Cuilcagh Mountain Park

Florencecourt, Co. Fermanagh ⊤028/6634 8855, ⓦwww .fermanagh.gov.uk. Mid-March to June & Sept 10am-4.30pm; July & Aug 10am–5pm. Adults £7, children £4, family £18.
A tour of Marble Arch's spectacular cave system lasts for around 75 minutes and commences with a boat journey on a subterranean river. Then you're led through a series of brightly lit chambers whose walls are bedecked with crystallized calcium and crisscrossed by mineral veins, marvelling at an astonishing array of stalactites. Bear in mind that you'll need warm and waterproof clothing and footwear and that tours may be cancelled as a result of heavy rain. Part of the Marble Arch Caves visitor centre is devoted to Cuilcagh Mountain Park (open access) whose shale-covered slopes cross into Co. Leitrim; displays cover the conservation of the park's bogland habitats.

Lough Erne cruises

Taking a **cruise around Lough Erne** is a splendid way to enjoy the waters and staggering vistas of its wooded and hilly shoreline. Several companies offer tours. **Erne Tours** ⓣ028/6632 2882, ⓦwww.discovernorthernireland.com, operates the *MV Kestrel* from the Round "O" Jetty, Brooke Park (just northwest of Enniskillen off the A46). May & June Sun 2.30pm; July & Aug daily 10.30am, 2.15pm & 4.15pm; Sept Tues, Sat & Sun 2.30pm; adults £7, children £4 (£1 reduction per person on 10.30am tour). From mid-May to mid-Sept there's also a Saturday cruise at 6.30pm to the *Killyheyling Hotel*, Bellanaleck (adults £20, children under 12 £15, senior citizens £19).

Castle Archdale Country Park

Lisnarick, Co. Fermanagh ⓣ028/6862 1892. Park: daily 9am–dusk; free. Centre: Easter–June Sat & Sun 11am–6pm; July & Aug Tues–Sun 11am–7pm. Free.

Set beside Lower Lough Erne, the park provides a host of activities and possibilities. You can explore the woodland, take lakeside walks or ride around in a rickshaw (£3 per person). Alternatively, bikes can be rented (from £3 for one hour to £10 per day) or you can take a pony trek (from £4 for a short ride to £12 for 1hr; discount for families of five or more). Boats can be rented on the lough (from £25 for two hours to £50 for a day). Alternatively, take the ferry to White Island from the marina (Easter–June & Sept, Sat & Sun 11am–6pm; July & Aug, daily 11am–6pm; adults £3, children £2) to visit the ruined abbey and its saucy sheila-na-gig statues.

Crom Estate

Newtownbutler, Co. Fermanagh ⓣ0870 458 4422, ⓦwww.ntni.org.uk. Mid-March to Sept Mon–Sat 10am–6pm (July & Aug extended to 8pm). Grounds and visitor centre, car or boat £4; National Trust.

The vast Crom Estate lies in a magical setting on the eastern shore of Upper Lough Erne. Containing the largest surviving area of oak woodland in Northern Ireland, it focuses firmly upon nature conservation and you can find information and displays on this and the estate's wildlife in the visitor centre. Fallow deer and the rare pine marten inhabit the woodlands and there are scarce butterflies too. Rowing boats can be rented to explore the lough and its islands and there are seven renovated cottages available for self-catering rental (ⓣ0870/458 4442, ⓦwww.nationaltrustcottages.co.uk).

Sports and activities

Adventure and activity centres

Corralea Activity Centre Upper Lough MacNean, Belcoo, Co. Fermanagh ☎ 028/6638 6123, ⓦ www.activityireland.com; **Lakeland Canoe Centre** Castle Island, Enniskillen, Co. Fermanagh ☎ 028/6632 4250; **Share Holliday Village** Smith's Strand, Lisnaskea, Co. Fermanagh ☎ 028/6722 2122, ⓦ www.sharevillage.org.

Bicycle rental

Co. Tyrone: Conway Cycles Loughmacrory, Omagh ☎ 028/8076 1256; **An Creagán Visitor Centre** Creggan ☎ 028/8076 1112.

Co. Fermanagh: Belleek Bicycle Hire Belleek Cottages, Main St, Belleek, Co. Fermanagh ☎ 028/6865 8181; **Lakeland Canoe Centre** Castle Island, Enniskillen ☎ 028/6632 4250; **Manor House Marine** Killadeas, Co. Fermanagh ☎ 028/6862 8100, ⓦ www.manormarine.com.

Boat rental

Manor House Marine Killadeas, Co. Fermanagh ☎ 028/6862 8100, ⓦ www.manormarine.com. Eighteen-foot boats which can take six people (half-day £50; full day £65) and larger "Skipper" boats which can carry eight (£70/£110).

Cinema

Enniskillen Omniplex Raceview, Factory Rd, Enniskillen, Co. Fermanagh ☎ 028/6632 4777; **Global** Oaks Rd, Dungannon, Co. Tyrone ☎ 028/8772 7733, ⓦ www.globaldungannon.com; **Multiscreen Studio**, Drumquin Rd, Omagh ☎ 028/8224 2034; **Ritz** Burn Rd, Cookstown ☎ 028/8676 5182.

Go-karting

Ballynahatty Fastrack Karting 3 miles southwest of Omagh, Co. Tyrone ☎ 028/8225 0170.

Horse riding

Co. Tyrone: Ashlee Riding Centre 4 Carricklee Rd, Strabane ☎ 028/7188 2708; **Carricklee Equestrian Centre** Urney Rd, Strabane ☎ 028/7188 3221; **Clanabogan Riding School** 85 Clanabogan Rd, Omagh, ☎ 028/8225 2050; **Moy Riding School** 131 Derrycaw Rd, Moy ☎ 028/8778 4440.

Co. Fermanagh: Drumhoney Pony Trekking Castle Archdale

☎028 6862 1892/07740508270; **Ulster Lakeland Equestrian Centre** Necarne Castle, Irvinestown ☎028/6862 1919.

Swimming

Cookstown Leisure Centre Fountain Rd, Cookstown, Co. Tyrone ☎028/8676 3853; **Dungannon Leisure Centre** Circular Rd, Dungannon, Co. Tyrone ☎028/87753 3252; **Fermanagh Lakeland Forum** Broadmeadow, Enniskillen, Co. Fermanagh ☎028/6632 4121; **Omagh Leisure Complex** Old Mountfield Rd, Omagh, Co. Tyrone ☎028/8224 6711.

Accommodation

Arch House Tullyhona, Marble Arch Rd, Florencecourt, Co. Fermanagh ☎028/6634 8452, ⓦwww.archhouse.com. Splendid rural guesthouse offering four spacious en-suite family rooms, fine food and a babysitting service.

Belmore Court Tempo Rd, Enniskillen, Co. Fermanagh ☎028/6632 6633, ⓦwww.motel.co.uk. Situated near the town centre, these modern self-catering apartments include two-room family units with a mini-kitchen.

Clanabogan Country House 85 Clanabogan Rd, Omagh, Co. Tyrone ☎028/8224 1171, ⓦwww.clanaboganhouse.freeserve.co.uk. Surrounded by spacious woodlands and its own tranquil gardens, this fine B&B offers food and very comfortable accommodation.

Gortin Accommodation Suite and Activity Centre 62 Main St, Gortin, Co. Tyrone ☎028/8164 8346, ⓦwww.gortin.net. Ideally situated near the Sperrin Mountains, this recently constructed centre features a hostel with family rooms and self-catering houses.

Muckross Lodge Muckross Quay, Kesh, Co. Fermanagh ☎028/6863 1887. Set by Lower Lough Erne with a beach at the end of its drive and its own swimming pool, this friendly B&B offers a babysitting service and has a family room.

Places to eat

The Linen Hall Townhall St, Enniskillen, Co. Fermanagh. Part of the Wetherspoon chain, this bar serves very reasonably priced meals and has a special family area at the rear.

The Mellon Country Inn 134 Beltany Rd, Omagh, Co. Tyrone ☎028/8166 1224. Near the Ulster-American Folk Park, this place serves a range of bar and restaurant meals, solidly reliant on local produce.

Oysters Restaurant 37 Patrick St, Strabane, Co. Tyrone ☏ 028/7138 2690. Exceptionally good fish restaurant, serving a range of fishy delights (closed Mon).

Index

Maps are marked in colour

U

V

W

XYZ